THE DIVINITY OF TRINITY:

JESUS CHRIST AS GOD

"A WEAPON AGAINST FALSE RELIGIONS"

EBHODAGHE DESMOND J. OSEZUA

PUBLISHED BY:

CHAPEL OF BELIEVERS PUBLICATION
Steilshooper Str. 281, 22309 Hamburg, Germany.
Email: contact@chapel-of-believers.de

First Published in 2014.

ISBN: 978-3-9816490-0-0

Cover production by Mister D. ankintemi@yahoo.com
040/29888221, Hamburg, Germany.

For enquiries and further contributions, please contact the author via: desygeneral@yahoo.com

ABBREVIATIONS

KJV - **King James Version**
NKJV - **New King James Version**
GNB - **Good News Bible**
NLT - **New Living Translation**
NET - **New English Translation**
CCC - **Catechism of the Catholic Church**

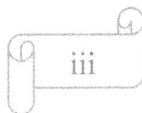

DEDICATION

This book is dedicated to the Holy Trinity: God the Father, God the Son and God the Holy Spirit.

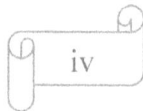

ACKNOWLEDGEMENT

My profound gratitude goes to Almighty God who has made the production of this book a dream come true. I sincerely thank Him for His blessings and protection before, during and after the production of this book. I must not fail to acknowledge the Holy Spirit who without His inspiration this book would not have been a reality.

I also wish to humbly express my sincere appreciation to all those who, in one way or the other, have helped in the making of this book a huge success. Those who read the manuscripts and made contributions by ways of suggestions and corrections, I am undeniably indebted to you all.

I also want to say a big thank you to all those who encouraged me morally, financially and otherwise in order to ensure the production of this book. I must confess your contributions are inestimable and invaluable. I am indeed grateful.

Just as you all have helped a great deal to ensure the production of this book, may God always be your Helper at the time of your needs. It is therefore my humble prayer that God would continually be above us to bless us, before us to lead us, behind us to protect us, beside us to guide us even within us to strengthen us, and that He would continually crown all our efforts with success in Jesus name, Amen.

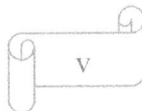

TABLE OF CONTENTS

PREFACE

In spite of the books that have been written by various authors at different times on the Divinity of Jesus Christ, one may wonder what necessitated the writing of a book of this nature. But when one realizes that a large proportion of Christians still do not believe that Jesus Christ is God irrespective of the sermons preached in the Churches, then one might consider it a welcome development.

This might be as a result of what is now called "selective belief". People select or decide what they want to hear and believe and not what the preacher preaches or they read from the Bible.

In addition is the fact that the Divinity of Jesus Christ is a mystery. And as a result, some people believe that it cannot be understood, discussed or explained. Hence, any attempt made in that direction is usually frowned at by them. They would rather prefer that the people wallow in ignorance and consequently, unable to defend their faith and beliefs when confronted by people with opposing beliefs thereby jeopardizing their chances of continuity in the Christian faith.

Some Christians see it as an unscriptural assumption made by the Church and compelled to be believed. That is, that Jesus Christ is God is not recorded in the Bible but assumed and taught by the Church.

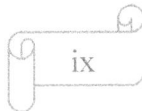

Born into a Christian family and from childhood, I have always been taught and believed that Jesus Christ is God. Way back in our primary school days, we used to sing hymns dedicated to the Holy Trinity. Thus, I had no problem believing in the Trinity.

Later in life, I got to know about some group of people whose main teaching denies the Divinity of Jesus Christ and consequently criticize vehemently and condemn the doctrine of Trinity. I was never surprised to hear them say Jesus Christ is not God. This is because I already knew what their mission is – to confuse and deceive Christians.

I got the shock of my life when I recently heard someone, who claimed to be a proud Catholic, say that Jesus Christ is not God and cannot be God. He went further to say that even if the Pope says it, he would not believe. Only then I realized how much damage those people have done with their so called "evangelism" and publications.

If any Christian would deny the Divinity of Christ, it could not have been a 'proud Catholic', because I know the Church (the body of Christ) has always taught and keeps teaching the truth, concerning Jesus' Divinity, that Jesus Christ is God.

I then decided to sample the opinions of some other Christians on the subject matter. I was again disappointed to find out that over 60% of them would quickly say: **Jesus is not God; He is the Son of God**. Just as many would still answer, if asked now. Some would say: "I don't

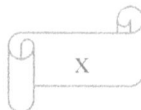

want to talk about it because it's a mystery." Only a few would at once say Jesus Christ is God.

I was really bothered about the responses I got from those people I sampled their opinions and thus, I was provoked in my spirit. This is because I expected every believer who is a Christian to have this understanding, that Jesus Christ is God; even when it might be difficult for a non Christian to accept this fact.

Thus, I was then convinced that there was an imperative need to write this book against all odds and without fear of being contradicted, to convict those who contradict, to enlighten those who are still ignorant and to encourage or strengthen the faith of those who already believe (Titus 1:9). Hence, the writing of this book with the help of the Holy Spirit, using the Bible as its main references, thus, a Biblical perspective of the subject matter.

My concern is that if Christians who are supposed to proclaim the gospel of Christ to the world that Jesus Christ is God, do no longer believe themselves, it means there is still a lot to be done even within the body of Christ – the Church.

This is because, it is only when one actually understands the true Divine status of Jesus Christ as God that one can fully appreciate who Jesus Christ was or is and what He did for mankind: The Creator becoming a Creature to die for His creatures in the hands of His own creatures. And

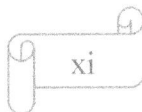

only then can we accord Jesus Christ the honour and worship that is due Him and everything that concerns Him.

The Gospel of Jesus Christ which we (as Christians) are supposed to believe in and preach to unbelievers, is that God sent His Son Jesus Christ who is as well God to this world, lived as a man and died for the forgiveness of the sins of the whole world. And that, it is only by believing in Him, that we can be saved (John 3:16-18).

It is in line with the aforementioned that so many prayers and songs are said or sung in the Churches today which apparently identify Jesus Christ as God. But the irony of it is that, after saying those prayers and singing those songs, some Christians would still contend vehemently that Jesus Christ is not God.

It therefore means that many of those "Christians" do not pray or sing those songs meditatively. They are either absent minded to listen to the wordings of the songs they sing in the Church or they just refuse to believe that Jesus is God. Some however claim they cannot find where it is written in the Bible, as they are quick to ask: where is it written in the Bible that Jesus Christ is God?

However, in Christianity, the belief that Jesus is God is not optional or personal. It is a "must believe" for every true Christian. In other words, the belief that Jesus is God is a prerequisite for every true Christian and it is the foundation of Christianity as a religion and what makes it unique or different from other world religions including Judaism, the predecessor of Christianity.

This is because, for us Christians, it is this belief that Jesus Christ is God that makes His doctrines or teachings supersede all other teachings whether the Laws, Prophets or Psalms which were also inspired words of God but fulfilled and modified by Christ Himself, giving us Grace in place of the Law.

Again, it is this belief that makes Christians worldwide to worship Jesus Christ just as we worship the Father; otherwise it would be an error to worship a mere mortal like us, if Jesus Christ were not God.

Remember God condemns the act of worshipping any other thing or giving the glory that is due to Him, to any other being, humans inclusive. It might be interesting to note that, we are not even allowed to worship angels who are heavenly beings and messengers of God (Rev. 19:10). Therefore, as Christians, we do not worship any other being besides God (Exodus 20:3).

The point here is that, it is due to the fact that Jesus Christ is God that Christianity, as a religion, worships Jesus Christ and gives Him glory and praises. This is mainly because He is worthy of our praises and deserves all the honour and glory even as recorded in the Bible (Rev. 4:11; 5:12-13).

But when one has been deceived and believes otherwise, that Jesus Christ is not God, he would only see Christianity as the collection of "False Religion" just as the Jehovah witnesses do. This is because, by the very act of worshipping Jesus Christ, an act which is exclusively meant for God alone, we Christians would have been committing the greatest sin against God.

This explains why a lot of Christians are being converted to Jehovah witness and other religions on daily basis, having been confused that Jesus Christ is not God. It however gives me a cause to worry due to the rate at which Christians are being converted globally. No thanks to this same group of people, who go about telling Christians that Jesus is not God thereby deceiving them and converting them into their religion.

An issue worthy of note here is the fact that we Christians are not doing well enough to properly inform ourselves of the truth. However, the word of God has warned that only the truth we know can set us free. It now seems to me that many people do not even want to know the truth. Else, how does one explain a situation even when Biblical facts are presented explicitly, and the people still do not want to accept these facts?

I was trying to drive home a point the other day with a fellow Christian, citing relevant scriptures to buttress my point. I was however shocked to my marrows to hear him say that whatever I said then would not make any difference to him.

That was because he already had his mind made up on what he believes and was not ready to change that, not even when what he believes, in that particular case, was contrary to the scriptures. You hear such people say something like: "nobody can tell me that; not even my pastor or priest can convince me."

This is just like what that young "proud Catholic" also told me that not even the Pope could convince him that Jesus is God. But the reality is that we can only worship God in spirit and truth and not in pretense as some Christians prefer nowadays.

Be that as it may, as a Christian, one must first firmly believe that Jesus Christ is God. All I have said so far might however still sound strange to those who had not believed, nevertheless, I encourage such to study this book with their Bibles and not just to read it, believing that the Bible is the inspired words of God, and therefore, our highest authority.

> *All Scripture is given by inspiration of God, and is profitable for doctrine, for reproof, for correction, for instruction in righteousness, that the man of God may be complete, thoroughly equipped for every good work (2 Tim. 3:16,17).*

One may also want to know, how this book is a weapon against false religions. But I feel the first question should

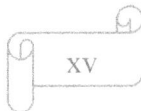

be: How do we know a false religion? For me, the answer to the above question is very simple.

Firstly, we know a true or false religion by what that religion teaches. In other words, it is the teachings of a particular religion that determine whether that religion is true or false. Therefore, a false religion is one that teaches false doctrines. Another imminent question would be: What is a false doctrine? False doctrines are the teachings or beliefs by some groups of people which are contrary to the inspired scriptures (the word of God).

And as you have just read from the above scripture: (2 Tim. 3:16, 17), such groups of people need to be reproved and those false doctrines need to be corrected using the appropriate inspired scripture. This is the primary aim of this book.

By so doing, we shall examine the contrary points or views which they hold and teach others falsely with a view to debunking them. Having said that, you will agree with me that, when we are able to understand scripturally that Jesus Christ is God, every other person or group of persons that teaches otherwise, can only be false teacher(s) for teaching false doctrines especially this, which has to do with a very sensitive and important issue: THE DIVINITY OF JESUS CHRIST.

CHAPTER ONE

UNDERSTANDING TRINITY

The Divinity of Jesus, as the Messiah, is unambiguously attested to in the whole of the scriptures. However, it can be somewhat difficult to comprehend the fact that Jesus Christ is God and one with God, unless we examine it from the perspective of the Holy Trinity.

This is because, if we believe or say that Jesus Christ is God, does it mean we have two or more Gods? Remember the Bible says there is only one God. Does it now mean that Jesus Christ is the only God? Or that He is God the Father Himself? In other words, since Jesus is God, does it mean when Jesus was on earth, there was no God in heaven considering the fact that there is only one God?

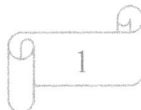

Does it also mean that it was God the Father who metamorphosed into the Son while Jesus Christ was on earth? These and many other questions might bother someone who does not really understand the doctrine of Trinity, when we say Jesus Christ is God.

And again, those who do not accept that Jesus Christ is God consequently find the castigation or disapproval of the Holy Trinity, the basis for their arguments. Therefore an understanding of the doctrine of the Holy Trinity is a basis for a better understanding of the Divinity of Jesus. In other words, the Divinity of Jesus is best understood in the Trinity of God.

At the same time, it becomes easier to believe in the Trinity when one is fully convinced that Jesus is God. In short, one cannot, as a matter of fact, believe in the Trinity when he does not believe that Jesus Christ is God. The reason for this is not farfetched. Trinity is based on the belief that Jesus is God. Therefore, once you do not believe in the Divinity of Jesus, there would be no basis to believe in the Trinity of God.

This is why I personally believe it would be rather difficult to talk about the Divinity of Jesus without talking about the Trinity of God or vice versa. Therefore, it becomes imperative to examine the doctrine of Trinity alongside the subject matter, which is the Divinity of Jesus Christ.

TRINITY AS A MYSTERY

The doctrine of the Holy Trinity is yet another mystery. However, by a mystery, the Church refers to **"a truth which is above reason but revealed by God**." It is a truth revealed by God meant to be believed by all who believe in God Almighty. Yet a lot of Christians and non-Christians alike do not believe in the doctrine of the Trinity. Even some, who claim to believe in the doctrine, do not understand what the doctrine of the Trinity is all about.

This is evident in the ways they argue unknowingly against the doctrine of Trinity. For example, someone who confesses the Trinity still argues that Jesus Christ is not God or equal with God. It therefore means that he does not understand what he professes in the first place.

This is one area I feel we Christians are not doing enough. A lot of Christians do not want to talk about the Trinity simply because it is said to be a mystery; and as such, it is strongly presumed that it cannot be understood nor explained just like the Divinity of Jesus Christ. But you will agree with me that it can be very difficult for someone to believe what he or she cannot understand or explain.

The question however is: How does one defend such beliefs especially when confronted by people, who have different or opposing beliefs, when he does not understand them himself? Your guess is as good as mine.

This, I strongly believe, is largely responsible for the ease at which many Christians are being converted to other religions, simply because they cannot defend firmly what they profess. My question here is: How long are we going to fold our arms and watch our fellow Christians being deceived and converted globally?

The point I am trying to make is this, that Trinity is a mystery does not mean we do not have to know what the doctrine is all about. In fact, most of the things we believe as Christians are mysteries even as recorded in 1 Tim. 3:16 (GNB):

> *"No one can deny how great is the secret (mystery) of our religion."*

Now if we agree that our religion contains amazing revelation (NET), does it mean we do not have to understand what we believe because they are mysteries? Just as I have earlier noted, that they are mysteries does not mean we do not have to know or understand what they teach or mean but that they are sacred secrets (truth) which have been revealed by God. The Church is very clear about this!

However, what baffles me most is that if we agree that a mystery is a secret that has been revealed, I would like to ask again, how secret is a mystery that has been revealed? I guess you will agree with me that a secret that had been revealed is no longer a secret.

So then, why do some Christians still hold these doctrines with upmost secrecy to the extent, some would say, they do not want to talk about them because they are mysteries? Maybe they believe they are called mysteries because they are too difficult to understand or explain.

On the contrary, they are termed mysteries because they were secrets which the people of old even in their wisdom could not know. This is because, they are above human reasoning. In other words, they are things man could not have known except for the revelations. For example, how could men in their ordinary sense have reasoned that in one God there are three distinct Persons? It was therefore a secret which was however later revealed by God. Let us consider here what Apostle Paul says about: Revelation of mysteries:

> *Now to Him who is able to establish you according to my gospel and the preaching of Jesus Christ,* **according to the revelation of the mystery kept secret since the world began but now made manifest,** *and by the prophetic Scriptures made known to all nations, according to the commandment of the everlasting God, for obedience to the faith (Rom. 16:25-26, NKJV).*

From the above scripture, you would agree with me that the mystery, which had been kept secret since the foundation of the world, has been revealed and made known to all nations. You would remember Jesus Christ

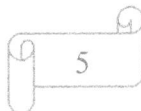

also said in the gospel that so many things which we now know were hidden even from the wise and the prudent in the past (Matt. 11:25; 13:35).

They were mysteries kept secret but they have now been revealed by God through Christ Jesus. Read also Ephesians 3:8-11. God has indeed made known to us the mystery of His will (Ephesians 1:9, NKJV).

Apostle Paul wasted no time in telling the Colossians that he became a minister for the purpose of proclaiming the mystery which had been hidden from ages and from generations, but now has been revealed to God's people (Colossians 1:26).

Now that these mysteries have been revealed, do we need to mystify or remake them mysteries or secrets? Rather, I strongly believe that all we need to do is to believe in these mysteries and try as much as possible to understand what they mean or teach. This is because, the more we understand, the better we believe. This is why I totally agree with St. Augustine who is quoted as having said:

> "I believe, in order to understand; and I understand, the better to believe."

Thus, it is important that we understand to some degree, the mysteries we believe in because it will only help us to believe more or better in these mysteries and to be able to defend same when confronted by people who do not

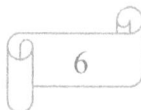

believe in them. The Scripture tells us in Ephesians 3:1-5, how God by abundant grace and through revelation made known to Apostle Paul the mystery of Christ which enabled him to write a lot about same, as we can now read in his writings. He again admonishes us:

> *That 'our' heart may be encouraged, being knit together in love, and attaining to all riches of the full assurance of understanding, to the knowledge of the mystery of God, both of the Father and of Christ (Col. 2:2).*

Apostle Paul here talks about the full assurance of understanding to the knowledge of the mystery of God. His use of the terms "mystery of God" comprises both of the Father and of Christ. No wonder he would say *"All I want is to know Christ ...." (Phil. 3:10, GNB); and nothing among you "except Jesus Christ and Him crucified" (1 Cor. 2:2, NKJV).*

We as believers must therefore seek consciously the understanding to the knowledge of the mystery of God through His words as recorded in the scriptures for the Bible says:

> *My people are destroyed for lack of knowledge (Hosea 4:6).*

Hence, Apostle Paul prayed:

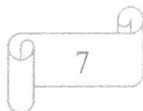

> *That the God of our Lord Jesus Christ, the Father*
> *of Glory, may give to 'us' the spirit of wisdom and*
> *revelation in the knowledge of Him (Eph. 1:17).*

Just as Paul would say: **I do not desire that you be ignorant of this mystery** (Romans 11:25, NKJV); but I pray, **that utterance be given to us, that we may open our mouth boldly to make known the mystery of the gospel** (Ephesians 6:19); **and to speak the mystery of Christ** (Colossians 4:3). Thus, we are supposed to know and speak boldly of these mysteries; hence, attempts would be made in this book to explain the doctrine of the HOLY TRINITY.

THE MEANING OF TRINITY

According to Oxford Advanced Learner's Dictionary (2010), Trinity is the Union of the Father, the Son, and the Holy Spirit as One God. This is a very simple and direct meaning of the term Trinity; three Persons in one God.

In other words, the term Trinity is used to signify the truth that in the unity of the Godhead, there are three Persons, the Father, the Son and the Holy Spirit, these three Persons being truly distinct one from another.

Thus, the Christian doctrine of the Trinity defines God as three divine Persons distinctly co-existing in unity as co-equal, co-eternal and consubstantial. According to this

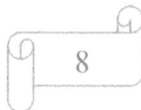

doctrine, God exists as three Persons but is One God, meaning that God the Son and God the Holy Spirit have exactly the same nature or being as God the Father in every way. Whatever attributes God the Father has, God the Son and God the Holy Spirit have as well.

Thus, in the words of the Athanasian Creed:

> *"The Father is God, the Son is God, and the Holy Spirit is God, and yet there are not three Gods, but One God."*

In this Trinity of Persons, the Son is begotten of the Father, by an eternal generation, and the Holy Spirit proceeds by an eternal procession from the Father and the Son. Yet, these Persons are co-eternal and co-equal: all alike are uncreated and omnipotent. This, the Church teaches, is the revelation regarding God's nature which Jesus Christ, the Son of God, came upon the earth to deliver to the world.

THE ORIGIN OF THE TERM TRINITY

It must be noted that there is no reference to the term "TRINITY," by which the three divine Persons are denoted together, in the Scripture. The word "trias" (of which the Latin trinitas is a translation) was first used about 180 A.D. to speak of the Trinity of God. It was however at the first Ecumenical Council held at Nicaea in 325 A.D. that the

Church confessed that the Son is consubstantial with the Father, that is, only one God with Him, considering the revelations from the scriptures (Michael E. Bassey, 1997). It was thereafter that the term Trinity became popularly used among Christians.

It must again be emphasized that it was not at that Ecumenical Council held in 325 A.D. that the Church confessed Jesus as God, as some people erroneously insinuate and propagate. The Church rather, inherited the belief that Jesus Christ was God.

That is, the belief that Jesus is God predated the Church but also led to the establishment of the Church. The Church, the early Christians then, were those who accepted that Jesus Christ was the Son of God or God in human appearance as expressed explicitly in their writing of the scriptures: **"The Word made flesh"** (Incarnation).

The Council was convoked as a result of the controversies put forward by a group of Arian Fathers led by Arius who held Arianism, a heresy that denied the Divinity of Jesus Christ. According to them, the Son is an inferior or subordinate being and unlike the Father. That is to say, He is not of the same substance with the Father.

They regarded Jesus as a lesser being to the Father and that He was created by God. These, and many other things they said, were contrary to what the Church believes and had taught about the Divinity of Jesus Christ.

It was in attempt to reconcile the controversies and restore peace among the Christians that Emperor Constantine convened the First Ecumenical Council in 325 A.D. by inviting Bishops, Priests, Deacons, etc. around the then Christian world. At the end of their deliberations, they came to the conclusion that Jesus is only one God with the Father, based on scriptures and revelations.

According to the Nicene Creed:

> *".... We believe in one Lord, Jesus Christ, the only Son of God, eternally begotten of the Father, God from God, Light from Light, true God from true God, begotten not made, of the same substance with the Father. Through Him all things were made...."*

Jesus is God from God and true God from true God. What was confessed at that Council was that, irrespective of the fact that the Father is God, the Son is God and the Holy Spirit is God, we do not have three Gods but one God. Thus, the three divine Persons distinctly co-exist as co-equal, co-eternal and of the same substance as one God. This the Church refers to as the mystery of the Trinity.

That the term "Trinity" is not in the Bible does not mean that the truth it represents is not in the Bible as well. Apostle Paul made reference to the term "**Godhead**" to signify the full nature of God, consisting of the Father, Son and Holy Spirit, as recorded in the Bible (Col. 2:9, NJKV).

According to Michael E. Bassey (1997), the word Trinity is not in the Bible because it is a term coined by the Church to express the mystery revealed in the Bible.

THE EVIDENCE OF TRINITY

The term Trinity may not have been categorically used in the Bible nevertheless, there are many evidences found in the Bible which apparently buttress this doctrine of Trinity. One can find places where references are made to the three divine Persons in such a unique manner that can only demonstrate Their peculiarity and unity.

The evidence of Trinity from the Gospels culminates in the baptismal commission. Jesus instructed the apostles to baptize in the name of the Father, and of the Son, and of the Holy Spirit (Matt. 28:18-20). If we are to carefully analyze the above statement made by Jesus, you will find out that His use of the singular form of the word "name" and not "names" implies that though these Persons are three, They have the same, and one name.

The use of the conjunction "and" shows that these Persons are distinct or separate from one another (the Father "and" the Son "and" the Holy Spirit) as against the Holy Spirit being God's active force and not a distinct Personality, as claimed by the Jehovah witnesses. However, in their distinctness, they have just one name as explained above.

Let us also consider the fact that Jesus did not say in the name of **God** the Father, and of the Son and of the Holy Spirit or in the **names** of **God** the Father, and of **God** the Son and of the Holy Spirit. He simply said "in the name of the Father, and of the Son and of the Holy Spirit." This clearly shows that they all belong to the same class of Divinity as God. Thus there was no need differentiating who was God and not God among them.

If we have believed that the Father mentioned here is God (as it was not mentioned in that statement), what stops the Son and the Holy Spirit from being God respectively, considering the fact that they all have one name and that we also know clearly from the scriptures that Jesus is God (as would be discussed later in this book)?

Yet, some Christians who do not know what the doctrine of Trinity is all about keep asking, where is it written in the Bible? I therefore urge you dear reader to get your Bible handy and read meditatively as we explore what the scriptures actually say about the relationship that exists between and among these three Persons: The Father, the Son and the Holy Spirit.

THE FATHER AS GOD

No believer or Christian has been found to opine differently that God the Father is not God. Otherwise such a person would not be regarded as a believer or Christian in the first place, but an Atheist, one who does not believe in the existence of God.

Therefore, there is no gainsaying the fact that God the Father is God and thus, does not need further arguments or explanations. The emphasis in this book is on Jesus Christ as God and one with God; however let us quickly look at the person of the Holy Spirit.

THE HOLY SPIRIT AS GOD

In the argument against the Trinity, some people do not believe that the Holy Spirit is God while some others believe that since God is a Spirit and God is holy, then God is Holy Spirit or Holy Spirit is God. Some others again believe that the Holy Spirit is God's active force and not a separate Person. In other words, they see Him as an influence or action and not as a Personality.

This could be mainly due to the fact that He is referred to as a Spirit, as His name implies: HOLY SPIRIT. Therefore, how can a spirit be regarded as a personality? They argue. They however admit or accept the Personality of God (the Father) but maybe they forget the Bible also says that God is a Spirit. As a Spirit then, is God a Personality or an influence? I leave that question for them to answer.

However, in the doctrine of the Trinity, the Holy Spirit is seen as a Person and distinct from God the Father. Therefore, in order to substantiate this doctrine, we must be able to understand scripturally that the Holy Spirit is a Person and that He is distinct from the Person of God the Father. The scripture says:

> For **there are three that bear witness in heaven: the Father, the Word and the Holy Spirit**; and these three are one (1 John 5:7, NKJV).

Thus, if the Father is a Personality and the Son (the Word) is a Personality, the Holy Spirit has to be a Personality in order for there to be three that bear witness in heaven.

Again, if the Father here is God and He is one with the Word and the Holy Spirit, and the Word is also God therefore the Holy Spirit has to be God respectively. This is very similar to the baptismal commission where Jesus instructed the Apostles to baptize in the name of the Father, and of the Son and of the Holy Spirit, indicating Their distinctness One from Another yet Their unity as one.

He is popularly referred to as the third Person of the Blessed Trinity. In Genesis 1:1, it is recorded that God created the heavens and the earth but in the second verse, it made reference to the Spirit of God. This means that the Holy Spirit was already in existence at the beginning before and during the creation of the universe.

It also means that although the Holy Spirit is from God, yet They are physically distinct from each other.

Prophet Isaiah referred to God and His Holy Spirit separately when he said, *"the people rebelled against God and made His Holy Spirit sad" (Isaiah 63:10, GNB).* Jesus Christ made this very clear when He said that the sin (blasphemy) against the Holy Spirit has no forgiveness (Matt. 12:31-32).

This, you will agree with me, He said concerning the Holy Spirit alone, for we also know that God the Father as well as Jesus Himself, is a forgiving Father (Isaiah 1:18, 1 John 2:1-2, 1:9).

If the Holy Spirit is not a Personality, can an influence or an active force be made sad (angry) or sinned (blasphemed) against? Or better still can an influence teach, remind, guide or lead, speak, hear and prophesy? You will again agree with me that these are qualities only persons can posses.

Jesus says:

> *And I will pray the Father and He will give you another Helper, that He may abide with you forever. But the Helper, the Holy Spirit, whom the Father will send in my name, He will* **teach** *you all things and* **bring to your remembrance** *all things that I said to you (John 14:16,26).*

The scriptures above clearly show that the Holy Spirit is a distinct Person from the Father. In the first place, Jesus referred to the Holy Spirit as another Helper. This means that there was already a Helper, which was of course Jesus Christ Himself, but because He was about going back to heaven and He never wanted to leave His disciples as orphans, that is, without a Helper, He then promised them of another Helper – The Holy Spirit.

This is one of the areas where Jesus Christ also compared Himself with the Holy Spirit as They are both Helpers. Besides, each time Jesus referred to the Holy Spirit in the Gospel, He made reference to Him as a Person and used personal pronouns, namely: He, Him and His and never as "it".

Smith Wigglesworth, in his response to the question: "Is the Holy Spirit a personality?" in his book titled "Smith Wigglesworth on the Holy Spirit" answered thus: "Yes, He is. He is not an 'it', not an influence, but He is a presence, a power, a person, the third person of the Trinity. That is the reason why the Lord said, 'when He, the Spirit of truth, has come, He will guide you into all truth' (John 16:13)."

The point made here is that the Holy Spirit is a Person and is distinct from the Father in the Trinity but however the Holy Spirit is from God and is God, having all the attributes of God.

Similarly, God had also promised through Prophet Joel that, on the last days He would pour out His Spirit upon all flesh... (Joel 2:28-29, Acts 2:15-18). However, it was the Holy Spirit the apostles received during the Pentecost in fulfillment of God's promise of pouring out His Spirit. Thus, the Holy Spirit is God and one with God for we have only one God.

If we have been able to understand that the Holy Spirit is God and a distinct Personality, what do we then say to those who teach otherwise?

On the other hand, the Bible also records that Jesus was born of the Holy Spirit (Matt. 1:18, 20; Luke 1:35), was filled with the Holy Spirit (Luke 4:1) and baptized with the Holy Spirit (Mark 1:8, Matt.3:11, Luke 3:16, John 1:33). All Jesus did while on earth was through the power of God the Father and the Holy Spirit (Acts 10:38).

THE SON AS GOD

Some Christians, even in Churches where Trinity is professed and believed including the Catholic Church, do not believe or agree that Jesus Christ is God or equal with God. Therefore, I would like to proceed by answering some basic questions about God and relate same to the Person of Jesus Christ. This will take us to the next phase of this interesting topic of discussion: who is God?

CHAPTER TWO

WHO IS GOD?

According to the Holy Bible Dictionary (New century version, 2003), God is the One who made the world and everything in it. Similarly, the Oxford Advanced Learner's Dictionary (2010) described God as "the BEING or Spirit that is worshipped and believed to have created the universe."

If we agree with these two definitions, for anyone to be God, He must have created the world and everything in it (universe), and is worshipped.

Let us quickly clear the aspect of worship. In the Old Testament, it is clearly written that God is to be worshipped and Him alone (2 Kings 17:36, Psalm 66:4).

Who is God?

This is why Jesus Christ said in Matthew 4:10:

> *"For it is written, you shall worship the LORD your God, and Him only you shall serve."*

Similarly, we also find in the New Testament that Jesus Christ was worshipped in His entire earthly life, right from birth till He ascended into Heaven (Matt. 2:11, 14:33; 28:17). Even the angels worship Him.

> *But when He again brings the firstborn into the world, He says: 'Let all the angels of God worship Him' (Heb. 1:6).*

Having known that Jesus Christ was worshipped and still deserves our worship, one may also want to know if Jesus Christ deserves equal worship or honour with the Father. Yes indeed Jesus Christ our Lord and Saviour deserves equal worship and honour with the Father even as He Himself attests to:

> *That all should honour the Son **just as** they honour the Father. He who does not honour the Son does not honour the Father who sent Him (John 5:23).*

Thus, Jesus Christ deserves all the honour, just as we honour the Father. The most important point here is that all Christians who serve and worship Jesus Christ, serve and worship the Father as well and together They are worshipped (John 12:26; Rom. 14:18). But he who does not worship, serve or honour the Son does not worship, serve or honour the Father. You cannot worship the Father without worshipping the Son!

If Jesus is not God and one with God, why would God approve that the Son be honoured just as the Father is honoured? Read Isaiah 42:8 and John 17:5. God said He would not share His glory with anyone else, yet Jesus speaks of the glory He shares or had with the Father even before the foundation of the world. What a revelation of a mystery! God can only share His glory with a fellow God and not with any man or idol.

THE CREATOR OF THE UNIVERSE

Genesis' account of creation records that "in the beginning God created the Heavens and the earth" and subsequently, He created every other thing through His words, when He said "Let there be ...." and "................ came to be," except man that there was an invitation to create, when He said:

> *Let Us make man in Our image and according to Our likeness (Gen. 1:1-26).*

Remember, as at that time, Jesus Christ had not been manifested on earth and that so many things which we now know were unknown to the people of old as earlier noted.

After Jesus Christ has been revealed on earth, what does the Bible say about creation? In the Gospel of John 1:3, it is recorded that:

> *"All things were made through Him and without Him nothing was made that was made."*

In other words, nothing in all creation was made without Him (Jesus). St John added by saying, the Word was the source of life and that the same Word became flesh (man) and lived among us (John 1:4, 14).

Apostle Paul, one of the greatest apostles and writers of the Christian scriptures, made reference to Jesus Christ as the one through whom all things were created, those in heaven and on earth, visible and invisible, whether power or principalities. All things were created "**by Him and for Him**" (Col. 1:16-17 KJV).

Through Jesus, God made the world (Heb. 1:2). However, many people do not understand what it means to say all things were created through Him or by Him. It simply means that all things were actually created by Him together and in conformity with God's will. He is the agent or means through whom God created the worlds.

*He was in the world, **and the world was made by him**, and the world knew him not (John 1:10, KJV).*

He created everything there is. Nothing exists that he didn't make (John 1:3 NLT).

Therefore, we can boldly say according to the scriptures that Jesus Christ is the Creator of the world or universe because there is nothing that was made that He did not make. He made them all. Having a clearer understanding of John 1:1 that Jesus was God in the beginning, it could also mean that both Genesis 1:1 and John 1:1 are referring to the same Person as the Creator.

Remember, that the Bible did not say in the beginning God the Father created the heaven and the earth, but simply said God created the heaven and the earth and Jesus Christ was also God in the beginning.

We Christians are quick to assume that, all the Bible says about God in the Old Testament refers to God the Father only. One may then ask: Where was the Son during all that time? Was He on leave? A good answer to that question can also be found in the same John 1:1. We are told that the Word (Jesus) was with God, right from the beginning. This means that He was always with God the Father and the Holy Spirit.

Who is God?

Again, a deeper study of the Bible reveals that the word God as used in the Bible could refer to the Father, the Son or the Holy Spirit individually or collectively. For example, reading the Old Testament, we are told that the Israelites tempted God in the wilderness and God punished them as recorded in Numbers 14:26-35; 21:4-6.

Apostle Paul's account, tells us that the spiritual Rock that followed the Israelites through the wilderness was Christ (1 Cor. 10:4) and went on to say:

> "... let us not tempt Christ, as some of them also tempted, and were destroyed by serpents" (1 Cor. 10:9).

In other words, Christ followed the Israelites yet they tempted Him, and were destroyed by serpents in the wilderness. Again, when you read the book of Hebrews 3:7-9(NKJV), you would find out that the Israelites tested and tried the Holy Spirit and saw His works for forty years in the wilderness.

Likewise, as earlier discussed, in Colossians 2:2 (NKJV) we read, "... of the mystery of God, both of the Father and of Christ". Here, the word God is used to mean the combination of the Father and Christ. Similarly, there are various things that were said by God or about God through the prophets that He was going to do which Jesus Christ personally fulfilled during His life on earth. For Example:

I will open My mouth in parables; I will utter
things kept secret from the foundation of the world
(Matt. 13:34-35).

This is an Old Testament prophecy (Psalms 78:2) but fulfilled by Jesus Himself. Again, we also know that prophet Isaiah saw Jesus' glory and spoke of Him when he prophesied (John 12:41).

Jesus Christ also makes us to understand better, that the Old Testament are scriptures which testify of Him and that Moses who is credited to have written the account of creation and the Laws, wrote about Him (John 5:39,46).

"For if you believed Moses, you would believe Me;
for he wrote about Me.*"*

You would also agree with me that the Person Moses and the other prophets of old wrote about in the old scriptures is God. But here is Jesus telling us that He is the One they actually wrote about. Does that not mean He is the God of the Old Testament as well?

Thus, it would be an error to reason that nothing was said about Jesus Christ as God in the Old Testament or in the Laws except that it was then an unrevealed mystery that has now been revealed in the New Testament.

Therefore, following from our initial definition of God as One who created the universe and is worshiped, Jesus

Christ is equally God and one with God, for only one God created us and we all have one Father (Malachi 2:10).

DOES GOD HAVE ORIGIN?

In the beginning, God created the heavens and the earth (Gen. 1:1). This is the first chapter and verse of the Holy Bible and marks the beginning of what we know about the existence of God. This means, as at "in the beginning" as recorded in that verse, God was already in existence. It would only take Someone who was already in existence in the beginning to create things in the beginning.

God has already been established from everlasting. Therefore, we know that God has no origin for He is the beginning and the end, the first and the last (Isaiah 41:4; 44:6)

DOES THE SON HAVE ORIGIN?

Thus, if Jesus Christ is God, it would logically mean that He too must not have an origin, because God does not have an origin. In the case of Jesus Christ, was it His birth on earth that brought Him into existence? The answer, you will agree with me, is NO. His birth did not mark the beginning of His existence just as His death did not mark the end of His life.

His birth was a transition from heaven to earth, as He would personally make references to the fact that He came down from heaven to earth (John 3:13: 6:38) and remember He also told the Jews that: *"before Abraham was, I AM" (John 8:58).*

His death, resurrection and ascension, was as well a re-transition back to heaven (Acts 1:9-11). On whether the Son has a beginning or not, a readily available answer is again found in the Gospel of John 1:1

> *"In the beginning, was the Word, and the Word was with God and the Word was God."*

Suffice it to say that "the Word" here refers to Jesus Christ for He is the Word of God (Rev. 19:13). He was in the beginning with God.

What John explained here is that Jesus Christ has no origin like the Father. He was with God, and He was God. This implies that from the very beginning there was a God (the Father) that the Word (Jesus) existed with, and the Word (Jesus) was also God (the Son).

These series of statement regarding the Word (Logos) in that gospel, build on each other. The statement that the Word existed "at the beginning" asserts that as the Word, Jesus Christ is an eternal being like God the Father.

The statement that the Word was "with God" asserts the physical distinction of the person of Jesus Christ from God as well as His union with God. The statement that the Word "was God" states the Divinity of Jesus, thus Jesus Christ was and is God. That is, at the very beginning, Jesus was already in existence as God and with God the Father and the Holy Spirit.

The reader, should remember, the scriptures also say that His going forth is from everlasting, He is the everlasting Father and He is eternally God. Can an everlasting or eternal Being have an origin?

Therefore, the Son like the Father does not have origin and They are both one God who existed before the world began (John 17:5) and are everlasting Beings. Remember also that Jesus Christ (like the Father) is The Alpha and Omega, the Beginning and the End, the First and the Last and the One Who is, Who was and Who is to come (Rev. 1:8; 22:13).

THE NAME OF GOD

Gods generally are believed to be supernatural or supreme beings that have powers to influence or affect human lives and every other thing in the universe. Religion is the belief in the existence of God or gods and the various acts of worshipping Them. It therefore follows that every religion has a God or gods.

The common name for all of them is god. Examples include: the god of thunder, the rain god, river god or goddess, the Roman god of war, the gods of Egypt, the gods of Damascus, the gods of Edom, the gods of Syria, the Hindus god, etc. This means that "god" as a word is not a name of any particular deity but a title given to deities or supreme beings. What then is the name of our God?

GOD AS THE LORD

So many names have been given to God by different peoples and languages. However when God called Moses and sent him to Egypt to liberate the Israelites, Moses asked God of His name saying: "when the people ask what your name is, what do I tell them?"

Moses' question was answered thus:

> *Moreover God said to Moses, this you shall say to the children of Israel: I the LORD the God of your ancestor, the God of Abraham, Isaac and Jacob has sent me to you.* ***This is My name forever*** *(Exodus 3:15).*

The emphasis here was on the LORD which was the only new name that was among those names. For Moses had known that, He was God and God of their ancestors (Exodus 3:13). This, God also substantiated when He said:

I am the LORD, that is My name (Isaiah 42:8a NKJV).

God told Moses that although He related with his ancestors but they never knew Him by His name LORD but by God Almighty (Exodus 6:2-3). Moses was therefore the first person to know God by His name LORD. Thereafter the name "LORD" or Lord God became the popular name of God. This explains the proliferation of the name in the scriptures. This name LORD has been translated from and into other names, including Yahweh, Jehovah, Lord of Hosts, Lord Sabaoth, Lord All-Powerful, Lord Almighty, etc.

Therefore, it will not be out of place to say in line with the scriptures thus:

"But as for us, the LORD is our God"
(2 Chron. 13:10a),

"...... the LORD is God; there is no other"
(1 Kings 8:60b).

"For the LORD your God is God of gods and Lord of lords, the great God ......" (Deut. 10:17).

He is the Lord of lords. In other words, the Lord of lords is our God.

JESUS AS THE LORD

At the beginning of St. Luke's Gospel, when Jesus was conceived but yet to be born, Mary the mother of Jesus visited her relative Elizabeth. As soon as she heard the sound of Mary's greeting, she was filled with the Holy Spirit and said in a loud voice *"......blessed is the Child you bear"* (the fruit of your womb).

Of course, the Child Mary bore in her womb was Jesus Christ. And interestingly, she continued.......

> *"But why is this granted to me that the mother of my Lord should visit me?"*

Again she said,

> *"Blessed is she who believed, for there will be a fulfillment of those things which were told her from the Lord" (Luke 1:39-44).*

Of particular interest here is the use of the word "**Lord**". Here the Holy Spirit through Elizabeth (for she was filled with the Holy Spirit) reveals that the Child in the womb is **Lord** and the One from whom the message came is **Lord** as well. Of course, the One who sent the message and here referred to as **Lord** also, is God.

Therefore the One who sent the message and the One who was conceived are One or alike as They are both

Lords. If we agree that God is Lord and that Jesus Christ is Lord as well; does that not show Their Oneness?

Paul tells us that the second Man (Jesus Christ) is the Lord from heaven (1 Cor. 15:47b). Again, the scripture says no one can say that Jesus is Lord except by the Holy Spirit (1 Cor. 12:3). It therefore means that when we truly say that Jesus is Lord, we are acclaiming His Divinity under the influence of the Holy Spirit.

Otherwise, one would not need the Holy Spirit to say Jesus is Lord just as the Jehovah Witnesses, who do not even believe in the Holy Spirit in the first instance, but merely call Him lord for the fun of it. Jesus is the Lord of lords (Rev. 17:14), thus, He is our God.

In many instances in the scriptures, Jesus was either referred to or referred to Himself as the Lord (Matt. 7:21, John 13:13). Early Christians viewed Jesus as "the Lord" and the Greek word Kyrios which may mean God, Lord or Master appears over 600 times in the New Testament with references to either Jesus Christ or God.

THE NATURE OF GOD

According to A Catechism of the Christian Doctrine (1971), "God is the Supreme Spirit, who alone exists of Himself and is infinite in all perfections."
Jesus said:

> *God is a Spirit, and those who worship Him must worship Him in Spirit and truth (John 4:24).*

As a Spirit, God is invisible, He is everywhere and He knows and sees everything (i.e. Omnipresent, Omniscient and Omnipotent). No man has ever seen God except Jesus Christ (John 1:18) because He is a Spirit. God told Moses, No one sees Him and live (Exodus 33:20).

THE NATURE OF JESUS CHRIST

Jesus Christ, the Son like the Father, always had only the nature of God, except during His incarnation but unlike the Father, Jesus also had the nature of man during His incarnation. Thus, Jesus Christ had two natures:

1. The nature of God

2. The nature of Man

JESUS CHRIST AS GOD

A lot of people, Christians alike, make reference to Jesus Christ as the incarnated Man only. That is, they see Jesus as that Man who lived and died about two thousand years ago and that is all. They do not care to know who He was and who He is. He was God but came to earth as flesh (man) and dwelt among men (John 1:1, 14).

Remember the Bible says He was in the beginning with God. This means that Jesus was not created by God but had lived in heaven as God from the very beginning with God the Father and the Holy Spirit, till about 2000 years ago when He incarnated. His period of incarnation was about 33 years after which He went back to God in heaven and lives forever as God.

Or do you think it is possible that Jesus who was God from the beginning would have gone back to heaven and be less than a God? In other words, if He was God before His incarnation, as recorded in John 1:1, He would have only returned back to heaven and remains as God forever because that is what He was and is forever.

It baffles me a lot to hear someone who reads the Bible and as a Christian argue that Jesus Christ is not God. The whole of the Bible is full of revelations of Jesus Christ as God. Jesus clarifies this Himself when He said:

".... all things must be fulfilled which were written in the Law of Moses and the Prophets and the Psalms concerning Me" (Luke 24:44).

All that is written concerning Him in the Law, Prophets and Psalms indicated that Jesus was the promised Messiah who was God but manifested in the flesh. Similarly, in Philippians 2:6 (GNB), Paul wrote that Christ always had the nature of God. Jesus was fully God and is fully God.

JESUS CHRIST AS MAN

Jesus Christ became Man when He took the human nature (soul and body i.e. flesh and blood) in the womb of the Blessed Virgin Mary by the power of the Holy Spirit. The human nature of Christ was mainly in His physical Being. He incarnated as a Man (1 John 4:1-2, Philippians. 2:7). He was like men in all but sin (Heb. 4:15).

As a Man, Jesus Christ was made a little lower than the angels just as the rest of mankind so that He could die (once and for all) for the sins of the world (Heb. 2:6,7,9). He came into this world to show us the way to God Almighty and to lead by examples. He then demonstrated and taught us several things including the following:

1. That no man is good except God (Luke 18:19), whereas He was good and He is the good shepherd (John 10:11).

2. That our will may sometimes not be God's will and that we should always pray for God's will (Luke 22:42), whereas He had come to do God's will (John 6:38; 5:30; 4:34).

3. That no man or angel knows everything except God (Matt. 24:36), whereas He is omniscient, all-knowing (John 16:30; 18:4).

4. That God is greater than all men (John 14:28), whereas He was God (John 1:1) but did not cling to His equality with God (Phil. 2:6).

All these and many others He said as a Man to identify with His fully human nature while on earth and to demonstrate or illustrate the perfection and the supremacy of God over all other beings.

However, the above scriptures have been the source of arguments for some people who now find them difficult to understand, and as a result, they argue that Jesus is not God. For example, they argue if Jesus is God, why did He say no one is good including Himself except God when someone called Him a good teacher?

But you will agree with me that Jesus Christ, of a truth, was a good Teacher. The Bible tells us that He is the good shepherd and that everywhere He went, He was always doing good, helping and solving people's problems.

We also know that He was without any sin. That He chose to answer that way did not and does not make Him a bad Teacher. Or what do you think? Do you think that He refused to be called "good" makes Him "evil"? If I guess right and your answer is NO, what do you think made Him refuse to be called a "good" Teacher whereas He was one? Humility!

They similarly argue, if Jesus is God and one with God, why was His will different from God's will as recorded in Luke 22:42? I can assure you that Jesus came to this world only to do the will of the Father who sent Him (John 6:38; 5:30; 4:34), and it could not have been possible for that to change suddenly because of the imminent suffering He was about to undergo.

Remember He had foretold His disciple about how He was going to suffer and die. That, He already knew even from the beginning and that, again, was the will of the Father which He came to do. You would remember that He had rebuked Peter for making attempts to prevent that same will from taking place (Matt. 16:21-23).

This was however so, to demonstrate to us that we should always pray for God's will in our lives and at all times, irrespective of the situations, just as He had earlier taught His disciples in the Lord's prayer (Matt. 6:10).

They again argue, if Jesus is God or equal with God, why did He say that the Father is greater than Him (John 14:28)? Even some, who believe that Jesus is God, find it difficult or impossible to believe that Jesus is equal with God as a result of this particular verse of the Bible and thus find it very difficult to believe in the Trinity.

However, the answer to that question is still found in the same Bible. I mean, why did Jesus not claim equality with God? The answer is simple and it is again because of His humility. That was why though He was God but did not cling to His equality with God according to Paul (Phil. 2:3-11).

Like I earlier noted, all those things, He said to identify with His human nature and as a humble and obedient Son of the Father, setting examples for us to follow. A closer look at the life of Jesus Christ on earth, would reveal that He lived a simple life of humility. So humble that He never wanted to show off His true Personality. On many occasions, He demanded to remain anonymous after performing great miracles and also forbad some others from revealing His true identity (Matt. 12:16; 16:20; 17:9, Mark 3:11-12, Luke 4:41).

However, in His human nature, Jesus was still divine. Paul tells us that *"For in Him dwells all the fullness of the Godhead bodily" (Col. 2:9 NKJV).* Another translation of the Bible puts it thus: *For the full content of divine nature lives in Christ, in his humanity (Col. 2:9, GNB).* Jesus had God's divine nature in His humanity.

The Man Jesus was in the form of God (Philippians 2:6 NJKV). That is, He always had the nature of God and He was like God in everything. The nature of God He got from God for He is the natural Son of the Father and the nature of man He got from His mother Mary. This is why Jesus Christ is referred to as the Son of God and the Son of Mary.

The Church confesses that Jesus is inseparably true God and true Man. He is truly the Son of God who, without ceasing to be God and Lord, became a Man and our Brother: "What He was, He remained and what He was not, He assumed" (CCC 469).

I believe it is the recognition of this fact that the Catholic Church refers to Mary, the mother of Jesus, as the mother of God (Theotokos), in order to quickly remind the Catholic faithful that Jesus Christ is truly God and Man and that both the human and divine natures of Christ are inseparable.

This is why I had earlier noted that if anyone would deny the Divinity of Christ, it could not have been a true and proud Catholic because by merely referring to Mary, the mother of Jesus as the mother of God, which I believe he also did, would have been enough to inform him that Jesus Christ is God.

THE ATTRIBUTES OF GOD

God is known to have so many attributes or characteristics. However, let us consider these three attributes of God.

1. Omnipotence

2. Omniscience

3. Omnipresence

OMNIPOTENCE

This refers to God as All-powerful and Almighty. Thus, God is able to do all things with no exception.

With God all things are possible (Matt. 19:26b).

OMNISCIENCE

This refers to God as All-knowing. In other words, God knows everything even to the thoughts of men. Before God, nothing is hidden. He is the God of knowledge.

For the LORD is the God of knowledge (1 Sam. 2:3).

The LORD knows the thoughts of man (Psalm 94:11).

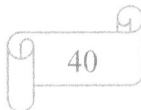

OMNIPRESENCE

This refers to the divine ability of God's presence to be everywhere at the same time. God is not limited by space, location or distance. He is in heaven but sees everything and His presence is everywhere.

> *"Where can I go from your Spirit? Or where can I flee from Your presence?"*

The Psalmist means to say here that God's presence is everywhere (Psalm 139:7-12).

DOES JESUS SHARE THESE ATTRIBUTES?

Every true Christian believes that Jesus Christ is God and as such automatically shares all the attributes of God. However, let us also examine if Jesus Christ had these attributes during His life on earth.

OMNIPOTENCE

Jesus was Almighty; there was nothing He could not do. He raised the dead, healed the sick, walked upon the sea and even the sea and the wind obeyed Him (Matt. 8:27). So many other things He did that no man could do.

> *What is this? What a new doctrine is this? For*
> *with authority He commands even the unclean*
> *spirits, and they obey Him (Mark 1:27).*

OMNISCIENCE

Jesus was full of divine wisdom. He was all-knowing including the thoughts of men (John 2:25). On many occasions, Jesus responded to the thoughts of His disciples and those of the Jews (Matt. 9:4).

The story of Jesus and the Samaritan woman as recorded in John 4:7-30 also confirms that Jesus was all knowing. Jesus also foretold things that happened at later times. For example: His denial by Peter (Matt. 26:34-35); His betrayal by Judas (Matt. 17:22); even His suffering, death and resurrection (Matt. 20:18-19).

> *Now I tell you before it comes, that when it does*
> *come to pass, you may believe that I am He*
> *(John 13:19).*

(Compare Isaiah 41:4; John 18:5-6).

OMNIPRESENCE

Jesus Christ, even while on earth, was not limited by location or distance. He could be in a particular place and see and know what was happening in other places at the same time. For example, the story of Nathanael as recorded in John 1:45-51 and that of Thomas as also recorded in John 20:24-29 buttress this fact.

> *"I saw you when you were under the fig tree before Philip called you."*

Whereas, Jesus was not physically there nor was He close to that scene. This greatly amazed Nathanael and facilitated his conversion and belief in Jesus as the Christ. Remember that Jesus Christ also said:

> *For where two or three are gathered together in My name I am there in the midst of them (Matt. 18:20).*

Could an ordinary man have done all these? Jesus was therefore omnipotent, omniscient and omnipresent and thus, He is God.

Who is God?

CHAPTER THREE

THE PROPHECIES OF THE MESSIAH AS GOD

The Old Testament of the Bible is made up of the account of creation, the fall of humanity and efforts made by God to redeem humanity. It was in the light of this that God promised His people the Messiah, the One who was to deliver His people, Israel. Consequently, virtually all the prophets of Old prophesied concerning the promised Messiah. Let us consider a few of the prophecies concerning Jesus as the promised Messiah.

The birth of Jesus was prophesied by Isaiah when He said a virgin shall conceive and bear a son and His name shall be Immanuel, meaning "God with us" (Isaiah 7:14). You would agree with me that this prophecy was only fulfilled in the birth of Jesus Christ (Matt. 1:18-23). However, when the Angel of God came to Mary and announced that she would conceive and give birth to the Son, the Angel also said that His name shall be Jesus (Luke 1:31). This God also confirmed in Joseph's dream (Matt. 1:21).

According to the prophecy of Isaiah, the meaning of His name is, God with us. From the onset, it was clear that the Messiah was going to be "God among men" as recorded in John 1:14.

> *But you, Bethlehem Ephrathah, Though you are little among the thousands of Judah, Yet out of you shall come forth to Me The One to be Ruler in Israel, Whose goings forth are from old, From everlasting (Micah 5:2).*

According to this prophecy, the Messiah would come from Bethlehem. Matthew 2:1 tells us that Jesus Christ was born in Bethlehem. Thus, Jesus Christ as the Messiah is from everlasting to everlasting.

> *'Behold, I send my messenger, And he will prepare the way before Me. And the Lord, whom you seek, Will suddenly come to His temple, Even the Messenger of the covenant, In whom you delight. Behold, He is coming,' Says the LORD of hosts. (Mal. 3:1).*

The Lord's messenger here refers to John the Baptist who came to prepare the way for the Lord as also prophesied by Isaiah (Read Matt. 3:1-3; John 1:19-23). "Prepare the way of the LORD; Make straight in the desert a highway for our God" (Isaiah 40:3). The LORD who says "I send My messenger to prepare the way before Me" or the LORD whose way was prepared (by John the Baptist) and eventually came to His temple is the Messiah – Christ.

> *They can see with their own eyes the return of the LORD to Zion (Isaiah 52:8b GNB).*

The America Standard Version puts it thus: "For they shall see eye to eye, when Jehovah returneth to Zion." Remember that no man can see God eye to eye and yet live. It therefore means that the Messiah who was to come, was the LORD or Jehovah but in the form of a man, so that the people could see Him eye to eye as He would come to His temple. Thus, Jesus as the Messiah is the LORD but manifested in the flesh.

In another of Isaiah's Prophecy, he said:

> *For unto us a child is born, unto us a son is given, and the government shall be upon his shoulder. And his name will be called Wonderful, Counselor, **Mighty God, Everlasting Father**, Prince of Peace (Isaiah 9:6).*

I need not tell or remind you that this, prophet Isaiah said about the Messiah that He would be called "**Mighty God**" and "**Everlasting Father.**" Why then do some Christians still refuse to believe that Jesus Christ is the Mighty God and the Everlasting Father? These prophecies came during the Old Testament when Jesus was yet to be known or seen and when God was regarded as only one true God. No one must believe, worship or serve any other god or gods apart from the only true Lord.

You shall have no other gods before Me (Exodus 20:3).

This God said about other gods not to talk of another mighty God. Yet, all these prophecies keep making references to the Messiah as Mighty God, Everlasting Father, LORD, and so on. All these only point to the fact that Jesus Christ is truly God.

The Jews refused to accept that Jesus is the Christ or Messiah because according to them, Jesus Christ did not fulfill the Messianic prophecy of reigning as an earthly King and returning the lost kingdom back to Israel. However, Jesus Christ made us to understand that of a truth, He is a King but that His Kingdom is not of this world (John 18:36, 37).

This explains why the Jews regarded Jesus acceptance to be the Christ, the Son of God as a blasphemy (Matt. 26:63-66). Thus they still await the birth of the Messiah till today. But again, some people who today say or believe that Jesus is the Messiah (1 John 5:1), have refused to accept the fact that Jesus Christ is God despite all those prophecies about the Messiah being the Mighty God.

JESUS AS THE SON OF GOD

It can be said that virtually all Christians, irrespective of the various denominations as well as the Jehovah Witnesses, believe that Jesus is the Son of God. However, not all can be said to truly understand what it means to say Jesus Christ is the Son of God. This is why I intend to elaborate on this topic.

Before then, I would want to believe that we have been able to establish some facts that Jesus Christ is God and was God. But to say that Jesus is equal with God, some people would still not agree. Their arguments may include the following:

1. Jesus is the Son of God.

2. God is His Father.

3. God is greater than Him, as earlier discussed.

4. If Jesus is God, Who was He calling His Father?

5. If Jesus is God, who was He praying to in Heaven?

Especially knowing that Jesus Himself had referred to God as His Father in heaven (Matt. 7:21). How can God (the Father) be equal with Jesus (His Son)? How can God (the Father) be one God with Jesus (the Son)? And so on.

Anyone who argues thus does not know what the doctrine of the Trinity teaches and may not have understood what Christianity is all about. Christianity is the religion that is based on the teachings of Jesus Christ and the belief that He was the Son of God (Oxford Advanced Learner's Dictionary, 2010). According to CCC 454, "To be a Christian, one must believe that Jesus Christ is the Son of God (Acts 8:37; 1 John 2:23)."

Hence, it is vital for every Christian to understand what it means to say "Jesus is the Son of God." Some other religions believe in God but do not believe that Jesus was the Son of God but at best, one of the prophets (Matt. 16:14). For example, the Jews (Judaism) did not believe Him when He said, He was the Son of God or that God was His Father, rather they regarded it as a blasphemy.

Similarly, the Muslims (Islam) do not believe that Jesus was the Son of God because of the implications but accept that He was one of the prophets and as such they regard Him as "Prophet Isa." They make references to the annunciation, the virginal conception and birth of Jesus by Mary (Koran 3:42-49), His disciples (Koran 61:14; 5:112), His gospel and miracles (Koran 5:110; 5:46).

However Islam rejects our Christian beliefs that Jesus is the Son of God, that He was ever crucified or resurrected or that He ever atoned for the sins of mankind (Koran 4:157). The Quran emphasizes that Jesus was a mortal human being who, like all other prophets, had been divinely chosen to spread God's message (Koran 2:136, 3:84).

Thus Islam refers to Jesus as "Isa" the son of Mary (Ibn Maryam), the apostle, servant, prophet and messenger of God, but never as the Son of God. According to the Quran:

> *How can He (Allah) have a "SON" when He has no "WIFE"? (Koran 6:101).*

However, some Christians who acknowledge Jesus Christ as the Son of God fail to understand what it means to say, Jesus is "the Son of God."

What does it mean: JESUS AS THE SON OF GOD?

This is very important because Jesus Christ either referred to Himself or was referred to, on many occasions, in the Bible as the Son of God or the begotten Son of God. Not only did Jesus refer to Himself as the Son of God or to God as His Father, God also confirmed this on two occasions in the gospel, where God referred to Jesus as His beloved Son in whom He is well pleased.

We have also found out that for one to be a Christian, one must believe that Jesus Christ is the Son of God. Then what does it mean to say Jesus is the Son of God? Does it mean that God is His biological Father: that God married a wife in heaven who gave birth to the Son? Certainly not!

This is one of the reasons why Islam has refused to accept that Jesus is the Son of God. "How can God have a Son when He has no wife?" They ask. They have refused to understand why Jesus is the Son of God or have refused to accept the fact that Jesus is the Son of God.

Jesus Christ, as the Son, was not given birth to by any woman in heaven neither was He created by God. He was Himself God and lived with God from the beginning till His incarnation (John1:1, 14).

In what sense then, is Jesus the Son of God?

If we agree even with our Muslim brethren that God does not have a wife and that God did not biologically father our Lord Jesus Christ, why then do we Christians refer to Jesus as the Son of God? Or better still, why did Jesus personally refer to Himself as the Son of God?

When Jesus said "I am the Son of God," He was speaking to an audience who heard Him, understood what He said and reacted according to whether they believed He was truly the Son of God or not. How many of those who argue that Jesus is not God or equal with God know that each time Jesus referred to Himself as the Son of God or called God "My Father," He actually expressed His Divinity and equality (being equal) with God?

The Jews, whether individually or collectively, refer to God as "Our Father" and that they are the children of God. For example, David and Isaiah made references to God as our Father. Watch these:

> *Blessed are You, LORD God of Israel, **our Father**, forever and ever (1 Chron. 29:10).*

> *Doubtless You are **our Father**, Though Abraham was ignorant of us, And Israel does not acknowledge us. You, O LORD, are **our Father**; Our Redeemer from Everlasting is Your name (Isaiah 63:16).*

> *But now, O LORD, You are **our Father**; We are the clay, and You our potter; And all we are the work of Your hand (Isaiah 64:8).*

None of them referred to God as my Father but our Father.

However, Jesus referred to God as "**My Father**" and that He is the **"Son of God."** He distinguished His Son-ship from that of His disciples by never saying "our Father" except when He taught them how to pray (Matt. 6:9). He emphasized this distinction by saying **"My Father and your Father"** (John 20:17) as against **"our Father."** They knew what He meant by calling Himself the Son of God or God, His Father.

Those who believed that He was the Son of God became His followers and worshipers (Matt 14:33), while for the Jews it was a blasphemy and thus they wanted to kill Him:

> *Therefore the Jews sought all the more to kill Him, because He not only broke the Sabbath, but also said that God was His Father, making Himself equal with God (John 5:18).*

The question is: How did Jesus make Himself equal with God for which the Jews wanted to kill Him? Did He categorically say He was equal with God? So what did He actually say? You may not have understood this very well. Let us read the same portion from another translation, The Good News Bible:

> *"This saying made the Jewish authorities all the more determined to kill him; not only had he broken the Sabbath law, but he had said that God was his own Father and in this way had made himself equal with God."*

You would have found out that the only thing Jesus said there, was that God was His own Father or calling God His Father. This was because by the very act of Jesus calling God His Father, He actually proclaimed that He was equal with God, which the Jews understood very well and as a result, were more determined to kill Him because to them, it was a blasphemy.

In a similar occasion, the Jews also wanted to stone Him. This made Him to ask why they wanted Him stoned (John 10:32).

> *The Jews answered Him, saying, "For a good work we do not stone You, but for blasphemy, and because You, being a Man, make Yourself God" (John 10:33).*

The question here again would be: How did Jesus make Himself God, as reported by the Jews? You would find out that Jesus did not say here that "He is God" but only said He is the Son of God. This again means that by referring to Himself as the Son of God, He again proclaimed that He is God, which the Jews understood very well but obstinately and ignorantly regarded as a blasphemy (Read John 10:36).

Also remember that this was the major accusation leveled against Him by the Jews that He made Himself the Son of God (John 19:7), meaning He has made Himself God. I want you to understand this very well, it was not as if they misunderstood or misquoted Him as claiming to be God or equal with God by saying that He is the Son of God or God is His Father because that was what He meant.

The problem was that they did not believe or accept that Jesus was the Son of God, but that He claimed to be (or made Himself) the Son of God, for they knew and understood very well that the Son of God is God and is equal with God. In other words, the meaning of "the Son of God" as at that time and in their language, was synonymous with being God and equal with God.

Thus, "how can a little boy of yesterday, the father and mother we know, claim that He is the Son of God (God and equal with God) when we know He is a man? Blasphemy! He deserves to die" (Luke 22:70-71, John 19:7). This was however in keeping with the Law of Moses as recorded in Leviticus 24:16:

> *"Whoever blasphemes the name of the Lord shall surely be put to death."*

Having a clear understanding of what He meant, He was then accused of blasphemy and sentenced to death (Read also Matt. 26:63-66). All these however took place in order to fulfill what had been prophesied in the scriptures (Acts 3:18).

Similarly, anyone who accepted or referred to Jesus as the Son of God was equally guilty of blasphemy. This is so because, by referring to Jesus as the Son of God, such was equally saying that Jesus is God, which was and is still blasphemous to the Jews. This explains why the early Christians were persecuted and killed by the Jewish Authority (Acts 8:1, 3).

Contrarily, some Christians who believe today that Jesus is the Son of God have refused to accept the fact that Jesus is God and equal with God. Some of them listen more to and want to imitate a group of false teachers who go about opposing the teachings and doctrines of Christ, using a single mistranslated verse of their Bible to criticize and condemn established Biblical facts.

According to one of the most popular verses in the Bible, John 3:16:

> *"For God so loved the world, that He gave his only begotten Son, whosoever believes in him shall not perish but have everlasting life."*

Jesus was not just a Son or an adopted Son of God but the begotten Son of God. Then, what does it mean to beget a son? The literary meaning of beget is to give birth to an offspring, one who has the same nature or image of his parents. For example, *Adam begot a son in his own likeness, after his image, and named him Seth* (Genesis 5:3 NKJV).

Both Adam and Seth were humans because Adam begot Seth. Now God has begotten a Son, yet they say, that Son is not God? For the Scripture to have said, "the only begotten Son of God," the author wanted to express emphatically that Jesus Christ is God. Whoever is begotten by God is God, just as whoever is begotten by humans is human.

I would like to ask a simple question here: what is the son of a lion? (a) Goat (b) Sheep (c) Lion. Sounds elementary but will help further in making the topic understandable. The son of a lion is a lion! Thus, the Son of God is God.

However, scripturally, the word begotten, and as used in that passage, does not mean "given birth to." That word begotten is translated from the Greek term 'monogenes' which means "only", "precious" or "unique in kind." Let us consider some other places where the word begotten is used in the Bible:

> *By faith Abraham, when he was tested, offered up Isaac, and he who had received the promises offered up his **only begotten son** (Heb. 11:17).*

Was Isaac the only son Abraham gave birth to? Isaac, of course, was not the only son Abraham gave birth to (read 1 Chronicles 1:28), but he was a precious and unique son, the only covenant son.

> *I will declare the decree: The LORD has said to Me, "You are My Son, Today I have begotten You" (Psalms 2:7, Acts 13:33, Heb. 1:5; 5:5).*

Does it mean that, the day the LORD said that, was the day He was given birth to or created, that is, if begotten only means to give birth or create?

I appeal to you for my son Onesimus, whom I have begotten while in my chains (Philemon 1:10).

Was Paul the biological father of Onesimus or did Paul give birth to Onesimus while in his chains? Therefore, the scriptural use of the word begotten does not only mean to give birth to a child but also to express a unique and precious relationship. Thus, suffice it to say that we as believers are sons and daughters of God but the Son-ship of our Lord and Saviour is unique and precious, one of its kind.

They even go as far as saying that Jesus being the Son of God signifies that He was created by God. This they buttress by citing the case of Adam being called the son of God in Luke 3:38 because he was created directly by God without an earthly father or parents.

Thus, according to them, the son of God refers to anyone that is created directly by God. If this is the case, why then is Jesus still referred to as the only Son of God? You will agree with me that if that is correct, it would be an error to refer to Jesus as the only Son of God because He would not have been the only Son of God considering the case of Adam. But that Jesus is still referred to as the one and only Son of God proves them wrong.

They again argue that Jesus being referred to as the firstborn over all creation (Col. 1:15) implies His birth or creation. However, we are told in the scriptures that

Jesus, who is the beginning, is the firstborn from the dead (Col. 1:18; Rev. 1:5).

If the use of the term firstborn is limited to 'the first to be born or created' in the scriptures, how do we explain that of Israel (Exodus 4:22), David (Psalms 89:27) and Ephraim (Jeremiah 31:9)? Therefore, Jesus being referred to as the firstborn does not signify His birth or creation but to emphasize His position as always being first in everything. Remember He is the First and the Last (Rev.1:8).

Some again argue that if Jesus is God, who was He praying to or calling His Father in heaven? This is a total misconception of the doctrine of Trinity. For in the doctrine of Trinity, it is believed that there are three distinct Persons in one God (the Father, the Son and the Holy Spirit).

Thus, when Jesus was on earth, the Father and the Holy Spirit were in heaven. This can be substantiated by the events that ensued at the baptism of Jesus Christ by John the Baptist in river Jordan. The heaven was open; the Holy Spirit descended on Him in form of a dove (from where?) and a voice was heard from heaven saying:

"This is My beloved Son, in Whom I am well pleased."

Whose voice was that? Of course, that certainly was the voice of God from heaven. Does the doctrine of the Trinity say that when Jesus (God the Son) was on earth, there was no God in heaven? Then where does that baseless argument come from? This shows that many of the critics of the doctrine of Trinity do not actually understand what the doctrine of Trinity means or teaches.

Among the Twelve, the one that was closest to Jesus or otherwise referred to as the disciple Jesus loved, is this same St. John. He stayed with Jesus till He died on the cross after Jesus had again demonstrated His love for him by handing over His mother Mary to him when He said "woman behold your son, son behold your mother" and from that day Mary lived with John in his house (John 19:26-27).

Little wonder then that John knew and wrote so much about Jesus' Divinity, which was his main aim of writing (John 20:30-31). He referred to Jesus on many occasions as the begotten Son of God (John 1:14, 18; 3:16, 18; 1John 4:9 KJV) and as God (John 1:1).

Some people do not understand that there is a difference between "the Son of God" and "a son of God." They misconstrue the Son-ship of Jesus as a son of God and not as the Son of God. For example, if someone says that he is a son of God, could that be regarded as a blasphemy? The Bible says:

> But as many as received Him, to them He gave the right to become Children of God, to those who believe in His name (John 1:12).

> *I will be a Father to you, And you shall be My sons and daughters, says the LORD Almighty (2Cor.6:18).*

Thus, if any believer calls himself a son of God, such a person has not blasphemed. Now I ask again, if Jesus had called Himself a son of God, would He have been accused of blasphemy? It was because Jesus called Himself or was called, "the only Son of God" and not "a son of God" that He was accused of blasphemy which is a capital offence to the Jews (Matt. 26:63-66).

According to the Catechism of the Catholic Church, 'Only in the Paschal mystery can the believer give the title "Son of God" its full meaning' (CCC 444). 'The title "Son of God" signifies the unique and eternal relationship of Jesus Christ to God His Father: He is the only Son of the Father' (CCC 454). It therefore implies that the title the **Son of God** means **God (the Son).**

Thus, Jesus being the Son of God does not stop Him from being God but that actually affirms that He is God. Some people who do not accept that Jesus is God would quickly tell you that "**Jesus is the Son of God and not God.**" They however do not actually understand what it means. It must be noted that the Father and the Son as used in the Trinity is meant to indicate the First Person and the Second Person in the Holy Trinity and not to demonstrate a humanly father-son relationship.

If you do not believe that Jesus is God, do not refer to Him as the Son of God. This is because you would only be contradicting yourself by so doing. Those who do not believe that Jesus is God do not accept that Jesus was or is the Son of God, rather they refer to Him as 'the Son of Joseph' (John 6:42) or 'the Son of Mary' (Koran 3:45) as the Jews and the Muslims do respectively, for they know what it means. The Quran again says:

Allah begets not, nor is He begotten (Koran 112:3).

The Messiah, Son of God is God

CHAPTER FOUR

THE REVELATION OF THE PERSON OF JESUS

Our Lord Jesus once asked His disciples and said: *"Who do people say I am?"* they replied, *"some say you are John the Baptist, some Elijah, others Jeremiah or one of the prophets."* Jesus asked them again *"Now who do you say I am."* Peter then spoke up *"You are the Christ* (Messiah) *the Son of the living God."*

On hearing him, Jesus said it was not his flesh and blood that has revealed that to him but His Father in heaven. That was because Peter invariably referred to Him as the living God. Just as earlier explained, to say Jesus is the Son of the God means that Jesus is God. In the same vein, to say Jesus is the Son of the living God means that Jesus is the living God.

This is so because, the prophecies about the Messiah had clearly indicated that the Messiah would be called Mighty God or God manifested in human form, as we have earlier seen. Thus, for Peter to have identified Jesus as the promised Messiah, only confirms the fact that Jesus is the Mighty God, according to the prophecies of old.

A lot of people do not understand the magnitude of that statement made by Peter. For if we were to look at it from the ordinary sense of it, what has Peter actually said? Of course the apostles had been with Jesus for some time before then and would have told them about Himself and His Father in heaven.

That statement would not have been "NEWS" that Jesus Christ is the Son of God and not to talk of it being a special revelation from the Father in heaven. You would only appreciate what Peter said when you put into consideration the commendation and blessings Peter received from Jesus for that singular act.

First He said "Blessed are you, Simon ...., you are Peter (rock) and on this rock I will build My Church, ... And I will give you the keys of the Kingdom of heaven and whatever you prohibit or bind on earth is prohibited or bound in heaven and whatever you permit or loose on earth will be permitted or loosed in heaven" (Matt. 16:13-20). What a shocking blessing from a shocking revelation!

Jesus Christ, on His own, also revealed that He was God by the various things He did and said, during His life on earth. For example, it is explicit in the Old Testament that no man can forgive sins except God (Isaiah 43:25, Luke 5:21). Not only did Jesus demonstrate that He had power to forgive sins on earth (Matt. 9:2-7), He also gave this power to His Disciples (John 20:22-23).

Some people relegate Him because He bears the Name JESUS. If His Names originally at birth were Lord, God, Jehovah, Yahweh; they would have believed that He is God. They should however remember that the Bible says His name, according to the prophecy of Isaiah, is Immanuel (God with us) but God gave Him a name that is above every other name, the name JESUS (Phil. 2:9-11, Rom. 14:11, Isaiah 45:23, Acts 4:12; 2:21). Jesus is Lord.

Let us also look at a few testimonies of the early apostles that reveal the true Personality of Jesus Christ:

> *"Now may **our Lord Jesus Christ Himself, and our God and Father**, who has loved us and given us everlasting consolation and good hope by grace,…"* (2 Thess. 2:16).

Here Apostle Paul unequivocally referred to Jesus Christ as our God and Father. For those who may not understand, the use of the word "HAS" in that passage shows that our Lord Jesus Christ, and our God and Father refers to only one and the same person (i.e. Singular Noun + Singular Verb). He also said:

> *Looking for the blessed hope and glorious appearing of **our great God and Saviour Jesus Christ**, who gave **Himself** for us, that **He** might redeem us from every lawless deed and purify for **Himself His** own special people, zealous for good works (Titus 2:13-14).*

Here Paul referred to Jesus as great God. Now, our great God and Saviour Jesus Christ who gave **Himself (**and not **themselves)** for us, that **He** (and not **They)....** This simply means he was again referring to one and the same Person.

> *And without controversy great is the mystery of godliness: **God was manifested in the flesh,** Justified in the Spirit, Seen by angels, Preached among the Gentiles, Believed on in the world, Received up in glory (1 Tim. 3:16, NKJV).*

Another translation (GNB) reads: "He (God) appeared in human form." Jesus Christ was God manifested in human form, compare John 1:1, 14.

And more explicitly, Paul wrote saying:

> *".... Of whom are the fathers and from whom, according to the flesh, Christ came, who is over all, **the eternally blessed God**. Amen." (Rom 9:5).*

Another translation puts it thus:

> *Their ancestors were great people of God, and Christ himself was a Jew as far as his human nature is concerned. **And he is God**, who rules over everything and is worthy of eternal praise! Amen (Rom 9:5, NLT).*

From these scriptures, it is very clear that Jesus Christ was and is God. Peter has this to say:

> *SIMON Peter, a bondservant and apostle of Jesus Christ, to those who have obtained like precious faith with us by the righteousness of **our God and Saviour Jesus Christ** (2 Peter 1:1).*

Jesus is our God and Saviour. It is strange to see that despite all these passages from the Bible, some people still argue, 'I will not believe that Jesus is God because it was not written in the Bible.' All we have read so far are not from the Qur'an but the Bible and the references are there. However, there are still many places in the Bible where Jesus is referred to as God. For example, Thomas, when he had seen and confirmed Jesus Christ after His resurrection, proclaimed Him:

"My Lord and My God" (John 20:28).

Jesus Christ did not rebuke him saying "why did you call Me your Lord and your God? I am not God, I am only but a man." On the contrary, that gave Him the opportunity to bless those of us who would not see Him but believe that He is "our Lord and our God." Yet some people still ask: Where is it written in the Bible? They should have said, "I will not believe unless God (the Father) has said it Himself in the Bible." Then read this. God Himself addressed Jesus as God when He said to the Son:

"Your throne, O God, is forever and ever" (Heb. 1:8).

What is the argument again; if God addressed Jesus Christ as God, who are we to say otherwise? Anyone who says he does not want to talk about it because it is a mystery, does not fully believe in his or her heart that Jesus Christ is God. He or she is only trying to shy away from the issue.

As a Christian who is fully convinced that Jesus is God, one must be ready at all times to talk about it and enlighten others, just as the early apostles did especially Paul, as we have seen in their writings. Therefore, when next you are asked, is Jesus Christ God? Do not even wait a second before you answer: YES He is God; because He is truly God.

JESUS' EQUALITY WITH GOD

On the equality of Jesus with God, I have earlier clarified that each time Jesus called God His Father; He expressed His equality with God or even when we call Him the Son of God, we express that same equality. In other words, to say Jesus is the Son of God is to say that Jesus is God and equal with God as earlier explained because He is the natural Son of God.

However because of His humility, He did not cling (hold on tightly) to His equality with God. Instead, He gave up all He had freely and took the nature of a servant, He became like human beings (whereas He was not). He was humble and walked the path of obedience even to accepting death, death on the cross (Phil. 2:5-8).

Someone again told me, during the course of this work, that he believes Jesus Christ is God but that He is not Almighty God. I personally believe that this is another way of saying Jesus Christ is not equal with God. However, according to the prophecy of Isaiah, as we have earlier read, we are told that He would be called the Mighty God.

If we say that Jesus is not equal with God, are we not as well saying that Jesus is not God? Can we say that Jesus Christ is God and yet claim that He is not equal with God, without committing the 'Fallacy of Contradiction?' The reason why Jesus is God is because He possesses all the attributes of God (see more explanations on Reasoning

Trinity in the next chapter) and thus Jesus cannot be God and yet be less than God (God is God).

If Jesus Christ is "**Mighty God**" and He again tells us that He is "**the Almighty**" as recorded in Revelation 1:8, does that not mean He is **Almighty God**? How then would a Christian say Jesus is God but not Almighty God? All these only confirm that many Christians do not really understand the Person of our Lord and Saviour Jesus Christ. **He is Almighty God**!

This is why I said one can only understand the Divinity of Jesus Christ in the Trinity of God. Jesus is only one God with the Father and the Holy Spirit. The equality in Trinity simply means that the three divine Persons (the Father, the Son and the Holy Spirit) are equally God who, together, make up one inseparable God. Everything They do, They do in common and everything They own, They own in common (John 17:10).

Thus, Their unity does not give room for such individuality and therefore there is no point trying to disintegrate the Divine bond that exists between Them for the Bible says They are one. Do not even try to disunite Them for They are perfectly united as One. See more explanations on Jesus' relationship with the Father.

JESUS' RELATIONSHIP WITH THE FATHER

Jesus Christ once said that no one knows the Son except the Father. Nor does anyone knows the Father except the Son and those He wills to reveal Him to (Matt. 11:27). The Bible also tells us that no man has ever seen God except Jesus Christ (John 1:18). So you cannot claim to know God more than Jesus His Son. Therefore, believe whatever He tells you about His Father.

Please read this scripture meditatively:

> *If you had known Me, you would have known My Father also; and from now on you know Him and have seen Him." Philip said to Him, "Lord show us the Father, and it is sufficient for us." Jesus said to him, "Have I been with you so long and yet you have not known me, Philip? He who has seen Me has seen the Father; so how can you say, "Show us the father"? "Do you not believe that I am in the Father, and the Father in Me? The words that I speak to you I do not speak on My own authority; but the Father who dwells in Me does the works (John 14:7-10, NKJV).*

Also read John 8:19.

To know the Son is to know the Father and to see the Son is to have seen the Father. Unfortunately some Christians do not believe in this Gospel rather they see it as a jest despite the level of sincerity demonstrated by Jesus in that passage.

If all Christians can just believe in the scripture, there would be no such arguments concerning Jesus' Divinity, because from the scriptures, it is very apparent that Jesus was God and is one with God. Having known that Jesus is a distinct Person from the Father, the above gospel to a very large extent, cannot but only buttress the Divine and inseparable bond that exists between Them.

In John 10:30, Jesus talks about the oneness that exists between the Father and the Son. In attesting to this fact that He is one with the Father, Jesus says:

> *If anyone loves Me, he will keep my word; and My Father will love him, and We will come to him and make Our home with him (John 14:23).*

Again His word says:

> *He who hates Me hates My Father also (John 15:23).*

To love the Son is to love the Father and to hate the Son is to hate the Father. Do not imagine that you can please the Father without pleasing the Son or worship the Father without worshipping the Son, rather, in pleasing or worshipping the Son only can you please or worship the Father who sent Him.

I am in the Father, and the Father is in Me (John 14:10).

All I have are Yours and all Yours are Mine (John 17:10).

The Father and the Son are perfectly united in love as one and cannot be separated by anybody or anything. Jesus in the scripture made this known: "**We** will come and make **Our** home." They are always together (John 8:29; 16:32), remember he who does not have the Son does not have the Father (2 John 1:9).

Just as Jesus Christ once told the Jews, He says:

> *If God were your Father, you would love Me for I proceeded forth and came from God (John 8:42).*

Again He asks:

> *Why do you not understand my speech? Because you are not able to listen to my Word (John 8:43).*

Hear Him still:

> *He who is of God hears God's words, therefore, you do not hear because you are not of God (John 8:47).*

Is anyone still interested in arguments? Let such read this:

> *If anyone teaches otherwise and does not consent to wholesome words, even the words of our Lord Jesus Christ, and to the doctrine which accords with godliness, he is proud, knowing nothing, but is obsessed with disputes and arguments over words, from which come envy, strife, reviling, evil suspicions, useless wrangling of men of corrupt minds and destitute of the truth, who suppose that godliness is a means of gain. **From such withdraw yourself** (1 Tim. 6:3-5).*

Having expounded on all these, I am convinced that for those who already believe, this would be a reassurance of faith. But for anyone who before now argued carnally and did not believe, if such has carefully read this book so far, and really desires to know the Biblical truth, I believe strongly that with the help of the Holy Spirit who is the perfect Teacher, by now such would have known the truth, that Jesus Christ is God, for it is the truth that sets free (John 8:32).

CHAPTER FIVE

REASONING TRINITY

The truth is that Trinity (three Persons in one God, Father, Son and Holy Spirit) is supposed to be a matter of faith; that is why the Church has referred to it as a mystery, meaning a truth, which is above reason but revealed by God.

However, because some of those who actually go to Church, lack faith which is the ability to believe whatever God has revealed, it consequently becomes impossible for them to believe in this sound doctrine.

However, attempt has been made in this book to explain scripturally the doctrine of the Trinity which Paul similarly referred to as Godhead in the Bible. Again, let us also see if reasoning can be used to explain the Divinity of Jesus.

Certain questions were earlier asked and answers given. Let us now look at some of the questions earlier treated. However, mind you when we say Jesus the Son is God, we have already affirmed that the Father is God. Thus I do not intend to prove that the Father is God because He is always God.

WHO IS GOD?

1.   If the Creator is God (Gen. 1:1), then God the Father is God, Jesus (the Son) equally is God (John 1:3, Col. 1:16-17).

2.   If the One that is worshiped is God, then the Father is God, Jesus equally is God. (They are both worshipped even together).

3.   If the Almighty is God (Ruth 1:20, Rev. 16:7), then the Father is God, Jesus Christ equally is God (Rev. 1:8).

4.   If the One who has no beginning is God, then the Father is God, Jesus equally is God (John 1:1 -2).

5.	If the One who lives forever is God (Isaiah 41:4), then the Father is God, Jesus equally is God (Rev 1:8; 21:6; 22:13).

6.	If the One who is "Lord" is God, then the Father is God, Jesus Christ is equally God (Luke 1:43, Phil. 2:11).

7.	If the Lord of lords is God (Deut. 10:17, Psalms 136:3), the Father is God, Jesus is equally God (Rev.17:14).

8.	If the One who is called great God is God (Psalms 95:3), then the Father is God, Jesus is equally God (Titus 2:13-14).

9.	If the One who is called the Everlasting Father is God, then the Father is God, Jesus equally is God (Isaiah 9:6).

10.	If the One who owns the throne or the kingdom in Heaven is God, then the Father is God, Jesus equally is God (Luke 22:30, John 18:36-37, Heb. 1:8).

11.	If the One who is to judge the world is God (Psalm 9:7-8, Mal. 3:5), then the Father is God, Jesus is equally God (John 5:22, 2Tim. 4:1, Rom. 2:16).

12.   If the Saviour of the world is God (Isaiah 43:3, 11), the Father is God, Jesus is equally God (Luke 2:11, John 4:42).

In case you never knew, Jesus is the King of kings, the Lord of lords (Rev. 17:14), the Alpha and Omega, the Beginning and the End, the First and the Last, the One who is, who was and who is to come, the Almighty (Rev. 1:8, 11), the Mighty God, the everlasting Father, the Prince of Peace (Isaiah 9:6), the Creator (John 1:3, Col. 1:16-17), the Saviour (Luke 2:11, John 4:42), the Great God (Titus 2:13-14), the only Son of God (John 3:16, 18), the Great Provider (Philippians 4:19), the Holy One (Mark 4:34; Luke 1:35), the Good Shepherd (John 10:11, 14), the bread of life (John 6:35), the Bright and Morning Star (Rev. 22:16), the light of the world (John 8:12), the way, the truth and the life (John 14:6), the great "I AM" (John 8: 58), the Author and Finisher of our faith (Heb. 12:2). Therefore Jesus Christ is truly and fully God.

The above I refer to as the Logical Proofs of Jesus' Divinity and oneness with God. In the Old Testament, all those divine characteristics were attributed to God alone as the only known God, because that was how He was known and as at then, the mystery of the Kingdom of God had not been revealed. But in the New Testament, Jesus Himself revealed the mystery of the Kingdom of God that had been kept secret right from the foundation of the world (Mark 4:11, Matt. 13:35; 11:25).

We find out that Jesus Christ possesses all those divine characteristics usually attributed to God Almighty alone. Then, the only logical conclusion will be: **Jesus Christ is God.**

On the other hand, some believe that Jesus is God but that He is not equal with God. Let us also see if reasoning can be used also to explain this.

A father and his son can be said to be one or the same in the sense that both of them are human beings but cannot be said to be equal due to the following reasons:

1. The father is older than his son.

2. The father gave birth to his son.

Considering the above, onc would be right to logically conclude that the father is greater than his son or that the son can never be equal with his father. However, in the case of God (the Father) and Jesus (the Son), Father- Son relationships, the above do not hold. Now let us examine them.

1. The father is older than the son: is God the Father older than God the Son?

2. The father gives birth to the son: Was God the Son given birth to by God the Father?

The answers to the above questions will demonstrate, to a great extent, whether they can be equal or not.

Firstly, we know that God the Father and God the Son both have no origin and have existed from the very beginning (John 1:1-2; 17:5). And this also answers the second question as to whether God the Son was procreated by God the Father (Rev. 1:8). Also see previous explanations.

We also have known that everything (visible and invisible) was created by God the Son and for Him. Therefore He cannot lack, for He is the Great Provider (Col. 1:16-17, Phil. 4:19).

Similarly, on wisdom and power of God, Apostle Paul writes that Jesus is the power of God and the wisdom of God (1 Cor.1:24). Also read (1 Kings 3:28; Matt 12:42; 13:54; 28:18). Remember, "Whatever the Father does, the Son also does in like manner" (John 5:19b, 21).

Having analyzed the above questions, it can be said that those variables of inequality in the father – son relationship, do not hold in the God the Father - God the Son relationship. Therefore, the only logical conclusion here again is that Jesus is God and equal with God. It must again be noted that the doctrine of the Trinity is not a matter of logic but faith, however, it is reasonable and that the titles, the Father and the Son, as used in the Holy Trinity do not connote our human understanding of father and son relationship.

JESUS AS THE SPIRIT

We have earlier noted that God is a Spirit and that Jesus Christ has the same nature with God. It would logically follow that Jesus as God would also be a Spirit except when He incarnated as a Man. In the light of this, we would consider some of the statements made by Jesus Christ during His life on earth which are being fulfilled today however in the Spirit.

1. *For where two or three are gathered together in My name I am there in the midst of them (Matt. 18:20).*

2. *When I go away, I will not leave you orphans; I will come to you (John 14: 18).*

3. *I am with you always, even to the end of time (Matt 28:20).*

When you examine the above statements critically, you will agree with me that Jesus could not have fulfilled those promises with His human or physical body. For example, how could it have been possible for Him to be present everywhere two or three people are gathered in His name globally with one physical body? Or how would He have remained with His Church even to the end of time with His human body? Those would have been impossible with a mere human body.

Since Jesus cannot lie, it means that Jesus, God the Son, is still present with us today, whenever we gather in His name, and even to the end of time, however in the Spirit.

No one has claimed to see Jesus Christ physically after His ascension (just like God the Father) with his physical eyes except through visions and revelations just as recorded in the book of Revelations by John.

The account of the conversion of Saul is another case study. Jesus appeared to Saul with his cohort on their way to Damascus where they intended to persecute the believers of Christ (Christians). None of them could see Him bodily. Rather, they could only hear His voice, as recorded in Acts 9:7. This means that Jesus appeared to Saul as a Spiritual Being and not physically.

More precisely, Jesus also portrayed Himself as the Spirit in the book of Revelation in that every letter sent by Him to the Churches ends with the words:

"He who has an ear, let him hear what the Spirit says."

THE HUMAN TRINITY

This can be used to explain the fact that human beings are composed of three constituents (tripartite): The spirit, soul and body and these three combine together to form one complete human being. Apostle Paul explained that the complete human being is made up of the Spirit, Soul and Body (1 Thess. 5:23).

For three bear witness on earth and the three agree as one (1 John 5:8 NJKV). This is the image and likeness of the Trinity of God in man. Just as three bear witness in heaven and the three are one, so also three bear witness on earth and the three agree as one (1 John 5:7-8, NKJV).

THE HUMAN SPIRIT

The spirit is the invisible inner being of a man. It is the part of a person that includes their mind, feelings and character rather than their body (Oxford Advanced Learner's Dictionary, 2010). Although the spirit lives within the body and has a lot of influence on the physical body, it is still distinguishable from the body. The body is visible but the spirit is invisible. Jesus says:

> *"God is a Spirit and those who worship Him must worship Him in spirit and truth."*

God as a Spirit would mean that God is invisible just as the human spirit is invisible. Thus when we always occupy our inner minds with the thoughts of God, giving Him all the praises and worship, then we can be said to be worshipping God in the spirit. Worshipping God in spirit has to do with sincerity of purpose as against hypocritical or "eye-service" worship. Accordingly, to be in the spirit, is to be very conscious of the things of God at all times and living out the life of Christ as a Christian.

The spirit is distinguishable from the body or flesh. Paul in admonishing the Colossians said *"For though I am absent in the flesh, I am with you in spirit"* (Col. 2:4). Jesus also distinguished between the spirit and the flesh, when He said the spirit is willing but the flesh is weak (Matt. 26:41).

Similarly, when the physical body sleeps and lays unconsciously, the human spirit sojourns on in the world of dreams. That is, it is the spiritual beings that one sees in dreams and not the physical bodies. However, whatever happens to the spiritual being has positive or negative effects on the human being.

For example, a child urinates in the dream and wakes up with his body wet of the same urine he probably urinates properly while dreaming. The encounter of king Solomon with God in his dream as recorded in 1 King 3:4-15 is an indication of how the spiritual realm affects the physical.

Therefore, although the spirit lives in the body, it is distinct from the body but has influence on the body.

THE HUMAN SOUL

This is similarly an invisible component of a human being. It also has similar usage with the term – spirit. They are sometimes used interchangeably. However, the word of God divides soul and spirit (Heb. 4:12).

The soul is the part of a man that does not die but lives on even after death and can only be destroyed by God in hell (Matt. 10:28). The soul can be said to be the gift of life God gives to a man when He creates him and He takes from him when he dies. Thus the soul is from God and returns to the Maker at death.

When God created Adam from the dust, he was lifeless until God breathed into his nostril the breath of life and only then Adam became a living soul (Gen. 2:7). At the death of that rich man who failed to acknowledge God in his wealth, God simply demanded and took his soul and the "fool" died that same night (Luke 12:19-20).

It is the soul that is accountable to God for one's deeds on earth and would be judged by God in heaven (Rev. 20:11-15). Jesus said:

> *For what profit is it to a man if he gains the whole world, **and loses his own soul?** Or what will **a man give in exchange for his soul?** (Matt. 16:26).*

Hence, there is the ultimate need to save one's soul from eternal damnation by believing in Jesus Christ and all He has taught us (James 1:21; Heb. 10:39; Matt. 11:29; 1 Peter 1:22).

John in his Revelation saw the souls of those who were slain and beheaded for the sake of God, living and reigning with Christ (Rev. 6:9; 20:4).

Therefore, the soul also lives in the body but is distinct from the body. Whatever a man does here on earth determines the eternity of the soul in the life after death. However, whatever happens to the body at death does not affect the soul. That is, irrespective of the kind of death one dies, the soul simply returns to the Maker.

THE HUMAN BODY

The human body encompasses all the parts of a man that are visible and tangible. It is also referred to as flesh or "flesh and blood." It is the human body that houses both the human spirit and the soul. God created the body from dust and it returns to dust after death (Gen. 3:19, Job 34:15).

The flesh the scriptures refer to as the carnal nature of man that desires the things of the world rather than the things of the spirit. *So then, those who are in the flesh cannot please God (Rom. 8:8). Because the carnal mind is enmity against God (Rom. 8:7).*

Therefore, though we live as flesh and blood, we must strive to be spiritually minded. *For to be carnally minded is death, but to be spiritually minded is life and peace (Rom. 8:6).*

The above illustration of the human trinity is intended to enhance the understanding of the Blessed Trinity. Just as the three components of a man combine to form a complete and one man, so the three Persons of the Blessed Trinity combine to form a whole and one God.

THE HOLY TRINITY

As earlier discussed, the doctrine of the Holy Trinity is a mystery. However, the mysteries that the Father is God, the Son is God and the Holy Spirit is God cannot be said to be the mystery of the Holy Trinity. This is because the doctrine of the Trinity is based on the facts that the Father is God, the Son is God and the Holy Spirit is God; based on revelations from the scriptures as we have already seen.

Nevertheless, what is usually regarded as the mystery of the Holy Trinity is the way the three distinct Persons, each being God, co-exist as one God. That is, the Father is God, the Son is God and the Holy Spirit is God, yet we do not have three Gods but one God (i.e. $1+1+1=1$). This unscientific and un-mathematical calculation of the Holy Trinity can be likened to that of the Holy Matrimony in which the man and his wife are joined together in love as one. That is $(1+1=1)$ as recorded in Ephesians 5:31.

> *"For this reason a man will leave his father and mother and will be united with his wife and the two will become one flesh."*

This is one area a lot of people do not really understand or misinterpret about the Trinity (three in one). Just like in Holy Matrimony, the man and his wife do not become one singular person upon marriage. They remain as two distinct or separate individuals but united in love as one family. I feel we should be very clear about this.

What the doctrine of Trinity teaches is that there are three Persons in one God and not three Persons in one Person. In other words, the three Divine Persons, Father, Son and Holy Spirit, make up one God and not one Person. I repeat again for the sake of emphasis, the three Divine Persons do not make up one Person but one God. They are distinct and separate Persons but united in perfect harmony and love as one God.

This is where a lot of people have over mystified the mystery. This has also led some people to untold imagination as to how possible it is for three distinct or separate Persons to be one Person at the same time. If three persons were to be put together to become one person, how would such a person look? How many heads, eyes, ears, noses, mouths, hands, legs, and so on, would such a person have? I guess they will also triple the numbers an individual has.

You will agree with me that this would not have been the case with God. How do you know that, you may want to ask? This again is very simple to answer. The Bible records that God created man in His image and according to His likeness (Genesis 1:26-27).

What that means is that God created man to look like or resemble Him. Could God have been such a "mystic Being" with multiple body parts and yet claim to have created man in His image? I personally do not think so nevertheless, your opinion may yet differ.

Still, the Bible makes me to understand that although we are all created in the image of God, but Jesus is the perfect image of God. That is, Jesus is the visible likeness or image of the invisible God. This means that if we were to see God, He would look like Jesus Christ. This can also explain why Jesus said, whoever has seen Him, has seen the Father. We therefore see God in the person of our Lord Jesus Christ.

To further buttress this point is the fact that we are told in the Bible that Jesus is now at the right hand of God the Father (1 Peter 3:22, Rom. 8:34, Col. 3:1) and not infused in Him or joined to Him as one Person. Also, in the book of Revelation according to John, he categorically described Them as being distinct from each other (Rev. 5:6-7).

Jesus never said He and the Father have one and the same body or that They are both one Person even when He said He and His Father are one (John 10:30).

Remember He also prayed that His followers may be one just as He and His Father are one (John 17:21-22).

Jesus could not have said that if He had the same and one physical body with the Father otherwise praying that all His believers be one **just as** They are one, would mean that all His believers should have only one physical body or become one person. This, you will agree with me, was not what He meant but to emphasize the need for perfect unity among His followers which now seems to have eluded Christianity as a religion.

My question here is: Where did that idea of the three Persons in one Person originate? This can only be another prank of the devil to confuse those who believe in the Trinity. You might not have understood the implication of this false assertion.

I have read somewhere about the argument of a group known as The Church of Jesus Christ of Latter-day Saints. According to its founder, Joseph Smith, in his revelation about God, he apparently saw distinct Persons who are individually God. Therefore, he concluded that there are three Gods. The Father, the Son and the Holy Spirit are each God and not one God according to the doctrine of Trinity.

Thus, he rejected the doctrine of Trinity which would have been a contributory factor for the formation of his movement, also known as Mormonism. If this is true that he had such a revelation in which he saw God the Father and Jesus Christ as two separate Persons, physically distinct from each other, would that have been a "news" or an issue? After all, that is exactly what the doctrine of Trinity teaches.

This, however, must have been as a result of the misconception of the "three in one's" formula. Maybe he would have expected to see a three-headed person or three Persons joined together as one Person as God, in order to believe in the Trinity. But is that what the doctrine of Trinity truly teaches?

Nevertheless, the doctrine of Trinity is very clear on this. They are three separate Persons, each being God and together They make up one God and as a result, we worship Them together in that perfect unity. Now, let us again examine the scripture below.

> *For there are **three** that bear witness in heaven: The Father, the Word and the Holy Spirit; and these **three are one** (1 John 5:7, NKJV).*

We can see from the above scripture that they are three distinct Persons; however, they are united as one God. God in this sense is a union of three Persons who are individually God. Even in the Old Testament when Jesus had not been revealed and God was regarded as only one BEING, He used the pronoun "US" for God indicating the plurality of the Persons in God as recorded in Genesis 1:26; 11:7-8. This is why The Amplified Version of the

Bible included: "…. Let Us (the Father, the Son and the Holy Spirit)…" in Genesis 1:26.

From the scriptures, we know that God is a spiritual Being and as such, is invisible but Jesus Christ was visible. Just as I have noted above, "Jesus is the image (visible likeness) of the invisible God" (Col. 1:15). No wonder it is written "No one has ever seen God except Jesus Christ who is Himself God" (John 1:18, NET).

Having realized and understood that Jesus Christ is God, does it now mean that we have more than one God? No is the appropriate answer because the Bible says there is only one God (1 Cor. 8:4, James 2:19, Eph. 4:6). The scripture says:

The Lord our God is one Lord (Deut. 6:4)

The Almighty Himself says:

I am the LORD, and there is no other; There is no God besides Me (Isaiah 45:5).

The scriptures above clearly buttress the fact that there is only one God; but God would again addressed the Son as God (Heb. 1:8). Jesus Christ also said, "I and My Father are one, whoever has seen Me has seen the Father." It therefore means that Jesus being God is only one God with the Father and the Holy Spirit, for scripture says the Three that bear witness in heaven are one (1 John 5:7).

According to Apostle Paul,

> *For now we see in a mirror dimly, but then face to face. Now I know in part, but then I shall know just as I also am known (1Cor. 13:12).*

It is only little we can know about God till we see Him in heaven and know exactly how He is. However, all we need to know about Him and in order to be saved so that we can see Him as He truly is, are all recorded in the Bible. Do not be deceived!

THE FALSE TRINITY

Some people, in attempt to confuse the believers, misinterpret the Holy Trinity as one of the false trinities of gods, claiming that the doctrine of Trinity is satanic. Therefore, it is important that we also take a quick look at some of those triads which the devil and his agents are using to confuse and deceive people about the true Holy Trinity.

The "triad" is a group of three gods who might be closely related and are worshipped together by idol worshippers as their gods. In other words, it is a grouping of gods or idols in threes. They are often members of the same families such as the father, the mother and their child or siblings. However, they are in triad and not Trinity.

A lot of triads have been identified around the world across history. They are so many that one may not be able to count. Among the ones in Egypt was that of Osiris, Isis and their son Horus. In Babylon, it was Nimrod, Semiramis and their son Tammuz. In India, there was Brahma, Vishnu and Shiva. The Greeks had Zeus, Hera and her child Hephaestus. In Rome there was Jupiter, Juno and Minerva. In some other nations, they had Thor, Wodan and Fricco. To mention but a few!

These and many others were triads made up of three gods who sometimes were believed to have quarreled and fought among themselves. These triads were sometimes broken-up and reorganized with different gods. They are sometimes depicted in an image form of tripartite beings, being worshipped as idols.

The Jehovah witnesses, in their attempts to confuse those who believe in the Trinity, would argue that Trinity is based on this arrangement of gods in threes. That is, Christianity adopted this same principle of having three gods, in the same manner as the idol worshippers. They would present a three-headed image in representing Trinity, indicating their insinuations about the Trinity.

From what we have read so far, in line with the scriptures, we know that the Holy Trinity is not a three-headed Being. Rather, the three Divine Persons in the Trinity are individually God but united in perfect love as one God. The Holy Trinity must never be confused with or mistaken for the triads!

CHAPTER SIX

TRINITY AND SALVATION

It was the divine plan of the Trinitarian God to save mankind after the first man had sinned and brought God's wrath and punishment upon all mankind. For it was out of the great love for man that God sent His only Son, Jesus Christ, to come down from heaven, show us the way back to God and to work out our salvation by sacrificing His life on the Cross of Calvary with the help of the Holy Spirit.

He instituted the new covenant which God had promised through His prophet Jeremiah (Jer. 31:33-34). This covenant is sealed with His blood which He shed for our salvation (Matt. 26:28, Luke 22:20). In other words, Jesus has already paid the price for our salvation. He has atoned for our sins and the sins of the whole world by His death on the cross.

However, what is left is our own part of the salvation, for everyone needs to believe in his heart and make confession with his mouth unto salvation (Rom. 10:9-10).

This implies that it is not enough to believe the gospel in the heart that Jesus is Lord but one must also confess same with the mouth. Therefore, for us to be saved, we must believe in Jesus Christ, for "He who believes in Jesus is not condemned" (John 3:18). To believe in Jesus Christ is to love Him and to believe that He is God; and to love Him is to obey all He commands us.

If you love Me, keep My commandment (John 14:15).

At the climax of His earthly ministry, Jesus instructed His disciples to go into the entire world and preach the gospel to all people and that anyone who believes and is baptized will be saved (Mark 16:15-16). And He said, baptize them in the name of the Father, and of the Son, and of the Holy Spirit (Matt. 28:19-20).

Thus for anyone to be saved, he needs to believe in the gospel and be baptized. And true baptism must be a Trinitarian affair, done in the name of the Father and of the Son and of the Holy Spirit. This explains why the Trinity was represented at His baptism in River Jordan by John the Baptist.

THE LANDMARKS OF THE TRINITY

These I refer to as some of the landmarks where God acted as Trinity in the history of creation and mankind.

1. The creation of Man (Genesis 1:26).

2. The creation of different languages (Gen. 11:7-8).

3. The Holy Conception of our Lord (Luke 1:35).

4. The Baptism of our Lord (Mark 1:10-11).

5. The baptism of the believers (Matt. 28:19).

6. The promise and presence of the Holy Spirit among believers (John 14:26)

In the creation of Man, God said; let "US" make man in "OUR" own image and likeness (Gen. 1:26). This means that it was more than "one Person" that was involved in the creation of man, for this was an invitation to other Persons. It again means that those other Persons this invitation went to should have the same image and likeness with God - OUR.

And in Genesis 1:27, it is written, *so God created man in His own image*. Now, what this means is that irrespective of the number of Persons that created man, They all have the same image and likeness according to which They made man and together They exist as God.

For those who argue that God was referring to His angels in that passage, I would like them to answer these questions: Does God have the same image and likeness with His angels, according to which He created man? Or do we humans (who God created according to His image and likeness) have the same image and likeness with the angels? The answers to the above questions would help in clarifying this assumption or argument.

Besides, the whole world at a time spoke only one language and as a result, they were all united and could do exploits. But God decided otherwise and said:

> *Come, let 'US' go down there and confuse their language, that they may not understand one another's speech (Gen. 11:7).*

Again, God used the pronoun US, (**Let us**). This means that God was not just a single Person considering the use of the pronoun 'us' by God and for God. And in verse 8 again, it reads *"So the Lord scattered them abroad......"* What this means is that, They came and scattered and at the end of the day, it was the Lord who scattered them abroad.

When it was time for the Son of God to be born, the Angel of the Lord appeared and announced to Mary that she would conceive and bear the Son, Jesus. The Angel made reference to the Trinity when he said, "the Holy Spirit will come on you, and the Power of God will overshadow (rest upon) you. For this reason the Holy child will be called the Son of God." This means that at the point of His conception, the Holy Spirit came on Mary, the power of God overshadowed her and the Son entered into her womb (Luke 1: 35,43).

Jesus Christ came for the work of salvation and that did not begin until His baptism. In other words, Jesus began his earthly ministry with His baptism. And at the scene of His baptism, the Trinity was present. The Holy Spirit descended in form of a dove, a voice of the Father was heard and the Son was physically there, thus the Father, Son and Holy Spirit were fully represented (Mark 1:10-11).

Jesus completed the work of salvation on the Cross of Calvary. And when He was about to give up the ghost, He cried out in a loud voice "Father into Your hands I place My Spirit" (Luke 23:46).

Also consider the number 'three' that surrounded Jesus' life. For example, His earthly ministry lasted for three years; He was denied three times by Peter; He was crucified with two others making them three to be crucified and Jesus in the middle. After His death, He was in the grave for three days. These and more others, I believe, also have some significance!

Jesus Christ ordered the apostles to baptize all those who believe in the Gospel in the name of the Father, of the Son and of the Holy Spirit (Matt. 28:19). Thus, our baptism as earlier explained is a Trinitarian affair. The Trinitarian God is invoked to signify the presence of the full nature of God or Godhead, consisting of the Father, the Son and the Holy Spirit.

The presence of the Holy Spirit among believers is a fulfillment of Jesus' promises to the Apostles that He would ask the Father to send them another Helper (Holy Spirit) who would stay with them forever.

> *Now, the Holy Spirit, whom the Father will send in My name......... (John 14:26).*

The Father, the Son (in My name) and the Holy Spirit.

Jesus told them further:

> *If I do not go the Helper will not come to you, but if I go away, then I will send Him to you (John 16: 7).*

This could also mean that Jesus Christ was the One who went to heaven and sent the Helper. Jesus also said when He goes, He will not leave them as orphans or alone, but He would come back to them (John 14: 18 – 19). After Jesus went to heaven, did He actually come back to the apostles? Or was it not the Holy Spirit that came on the day of Pentecost? Let us again carefully examine these three statements made by Jesus Christ:

1. If I go away, the Father will send you the Holy Spirit in My name.

2. If I go away, I will send you the Holy Spirit.

3. If I go away, I will come back to you.

Does it now mean that Jesus Christ was mixing words or He did not know what He was saying? Far from the truth, He is omniscient, all knowing; He only demonstrated the relationship that exists between and among them, for they are the same and one God.

THE DOCTRINE OF TRINITY VERSUS FALSE WITNESSES

The word doctrine is derived from the Latin 'docere' which means to teach. The Bible shows that a doctrine is a standard teaching which Jesus received from the Father (John 7:16-17 NKJV) and taught His disciples and also instructed them to preach same to all believers (Matt. 28:18-20). Therefore, that a belief is referred to as a doctrine does not mean that it wasn't Jesus' teaching.

Whether such doctrines are written down or not does not make them false. After all, not everything Jesus Christ taught or did was recorded. Apostle Paul admonished the Thessalonians that they should stand fast and hold the traditions which they were been taught whether by words of mouth or by letters (2 Thess. 2:15). This means that, not all the doctrines were in written form at a time.

The Blessed Trinity is one of the sound doctrines which some people will not endure but according to their own desires, heap up teachers for themselves that will turn the ears away from the truth (2 Tim.4:2-4).

It is called a doctrine because the Blessed Trinity is a belief held and taught by the church of God. It is a sound doctrine because it is based on the word of God. However a lot of people still keep asking so many questions. Even if you tell them, they would not listen because their predisposed minds are already made up. The Bible says, you shall know the truth, and the truth will set you free.

> *Beware lest anyone cheat you through philosophy and empty deceit according to the basic principles of the world, and not according to Christ (Col. 2:8).*

Some people who go around looking for Christians to deceive would tell you that Jesus is not God or there is nothing like the Trinity, using their human philosophy: If Jesus is God, why this..., why that...? Where is it in the Bible? And so on. There is the need therefore for every child of God to be armed against those tricks of the devil just as Peter counseled: Be ready to defend the hope you have in you at any time (1 Peter 3:15).

Do not be deceived for they are the anti-Christ spoken of beforehand. They are against the teachings of Christ. The Bible says:

Therefore by their fruit you will know them (Matt. 7:20).

And remember not all who say Lord, Lord, worship God and thus will enter His kingdom. For example, Jesus Christ categorically taught His disciples and the Bible also records among others, the following:

1. That He was going to prepare a place for us in heaven and then take us to heaven (John 14:3; 12:26; 17:24, Matt. 4:17).

   Yet they claim they are not going to heaven.

2. That hell fire is real and one should try to avoid it by all means (Mark 9:43-48, Matt. 5:22, 29, 30; Matt. 18:9, Luke 12:4-5, Rev. 20:10; 21:8).

   Yet they claim there is no hell fire.

3. That the soul does not die but can only be destroyed by God in hell (Matt. 10:28, Luke 12:4-5).

   Yet they claim that the soul is the same as the body and dies as the body dies.

4. Bible records that Jesus carried his cross and was crucified (John 19:17-18).

    Yet they claim Jesus was never crucified but hanged on a torture stake.

5. That those who believe in Him would work miracles in His Name (John 14:12; Mark 16:17-18).

    Yet they do not believe in miracles but claim that the days of miracles are over.

6. The Bible teaches that this earth will be destroyed and a new earth, the New Jerusalem will come from heaven (2 Peter 3:7-10, Rev. 21:1-2; 3:12).

    Yet they claim this earth will last forever.

7. Jesus founded His Church on earth as a community of His worshippers known as Christians/Christianity (Matt. 16:18; 18:17).

    Yet they claim that Christianity/Christendom is a collection of world false religions.

8. Jesus said He would be with His Church till the end of time (Matt. 28:20).

    Yet they claim that true Christianity died at the death of the last apostles but only resurrected with them in the 19th Century.

9. The Bible records that when Jesus resurrected, His tomb was empty (Mark 16:6, Matt. 28:6).

    Yet they claim Jesus did not resurrect with His body but only the Spirit (Luke 24:36-39).

10. The Bible records that the Son was with the Father from the beginning and both were God (John 1:1-2).

    Yet they claim that the Son was never God and that He was created by the Father.

11. Jesus said no one knows the time the world will come to an end (Mark 13:32).

    Yet they have kept predicting the end of the world falsely since 1914.

12. The Bible records that Jesus was worshipped right from His birth till He ascended into heaven as earlier discussed.

    Yet they claim that they cannot or do not worship Jesus Christ. This is because they argue that Jesus is a man, or at best, a god or an angel and not God and thus, does not deserve worship nor is He worthy.

13. The Bible, in so many places, makes references to the Judgment day and that Jesus will come again to

judge the world, both the living and the dead (John 5:22, Rom. 2:12&16, 2 Tim. 4:1, 1 Peter 4:5, Heb. 10:30, Rev. 20:12-13).

Yet they again claim that there is nothing like judgment or the judgment day. That God is not going to judge anybody based on his or her past deeds. According to them, when someone is dead, all his sins are forgiven, misquoting and misinterpreting what Paul said in Romans 6:7.

"For who has died has been freed from sin"

What Paul said there has nothing to do with the judgment day but repentance from sins. If you want to get a clearer understanding of what he meant, you would need to read the whole of Romans chapter 6.

14. The Bible records that the number of people going to heaven from all nations or tribes is uncountable (Rev. 7:9-10).

Yet they claim that only 144,000 people are going to heaven misinterpreting again Rev.7:4. What surprises me most is that, this is recorded in the same chapter of the Bible. They also believe that some of them are among the 144,000 people going to heaven, whereas the Bible clearly states the composition of that 144,000 which are only from the twelve tribes of Israel. What I do not understand is, if they too are from the tribes of Israel.

Conclusively, having failed in their prediction of the end of the world which they said would take place in 1914; they again claimed that satan was cast out from heaven to earth in 1914 fulfilling the Biblical revelation as recorded in Revelation 12:9. What a self consolation!

According to them, satan and his angels (demons) were cast out of heaven only in 1914. That would mean that satan and his angels were still in heaven right from their creation till 1914. Therefore, does it mean Jesus left satan in heaven, came to earth and was casting out the same demons and after His resurrection, ascended back to heaven and lived with them in heaven till 1914? How reasonable can that be? To drive my point further home, I will recommend that the reader, read 2 Peter 2:4.

Now, considering the above facts from the Bible, I want you to judge for yourself: This set of people, are they for Christ or against Christ? Is it the same Christ that we preach, they preach? Or is it the same Bible that we read, they read?

One may be quick to remind me that the same Bible asks us not to judge, so why then do we have to judge them? However, the interpretation of that Biblical passage does not apply here because the Bible clearly says by their fruits you will know them.

A bad tree cannot bring forth good fruits neither can you expect grapes from thorns. In the same vein, you know a false preacher or teacher by what he preaches or teaches. Having known a false religion based on the false doctrines it teaches, as we have seen from the aforementioned scriptures above, it would only be a case of calling a spade, a spade and not being judgmental.

How many of the Christians who entertain those set of people in their homes today, know that they do not regard themselves as Christians rather they regard our Christianity as the collection of false religion?

They have their own religion but hide under the guise of "true religion" or "true Christianity" just to deceive people. Their main objective is to wipe out Christianity. My question is, why do they not go to the Muslims, Jews and other religions or even pagans to preach their own religion and leave Christians alone?

Why is Christianity their target? As I wondered on those questions, only then I realized that they do not have much to say to the Muslims or other religions because they have the same belief concerning the Divinity of Jesus Christ. But to the Christians, they can convince and confuse that Jesus is not God, which is their primary assignment.

For me, it is even better to listen to a Muslim preach than to a "Jehovah Witness." This is because, as the Muslim preaches, you already know he would be talking about a different man called Muhammad and Allah, their prophet and their God, citing the Quran, which we Christians do not really believe in.

This group I am talking about here is however dangerous because they come under the guise of Christianity. They claim we read the same Bible, believe in the same God (Jehovah) and preach the same Christ as the "Son of God." Little does the unsuspecting Christian know that they are out to deceive him but gradually!

They start by making him believe that we actually read the same Bible and believe in the same God. This they do by, firstly, reading portions of their bible that correspond with our Bible, thereby making the would-be confused and converted Christian to believe that the Bibles are the same. They pay him regular visits where they study their bible together and give him some of their publications to read as well.

Having won his confidence, they proceed to more sensitive areas even when these are now different from what is in his original Bible, it might be too late for him to discover, because they would have given him a free copy of their bible to read from, which he now has confidence in. All of a sudden, he chooses to believe what he now reads from this their mistranslated bible than to believe in what he knew and read from the real Christian Bible. What a pity!

A lot of people have already been deceived by similar means and the way they dress gorgeously and erroneously quote their biased mis-translated so called 'bible', but do not actually know what they have gone into.

Their bible was only translated to suit their beliefs. This they did by either removing or altering all the places in the Bible that do not support what they believe and preach to others. For example, because they do not believe or accept that Jesus is God, they either removed completely or altered such areas in the Bible that indicated directly or indirectly but apparently that Jesus Christ is God.

Take for example, in John 1:1, it is recorded thus: *"and the Word was **God.**"* But in their bible it reads: "and the Word was **a god**." In Hebrews 1:8, we have: ***"Your throne, O God, is forever and ever"*** but their bible reads "**God is your throne forever and ever**" just to mention but a few. Now considering the latter, that is Hebrew 1:8, what do they mean by God is your throne forever and ever? Does that actually make real sense compared to our version? How could God have been Jesus' throne? They however chose to render their translation thus in order to conceal the truth.

It may however interest you to know that they are actually said to have started as a group of Bible students studying the Bible together in the United States. But it is again strange to find out that the Bible they studied is the same Bible we can read today as they are said to have used the

King James Version of the Bible prior to the release of their own translation.

Therefore, permit me to ask this question: Where on earth did they get those doctrines from, which they now hold and teach others falsely, which are contrary to the scriptures as recorded in the King James Version? Those can only be from the pit of hell and not even from this earth!

They cannot say that it is from their bible because as at their inception and early years from 1870s, they did not have their own bible when the Jehovah Witness founder, Charles Taze Russell, formulated and decided what their doctrines would be.

They were only able to print or produce their bible after so many years of their operation, between 1950 (the New Testament) and 1960 (the Old Testament) which culminated in the release of their complete bible as a single volume, known as the New World Translation of the Holy Scriptures, in 1961.

This translation was however done in line with their beliefs. In other words, their bible did not form or shape their beliefs but rather their bible was formed and shaped according to what they had believed. This is so because, before their bible was released between 1950 and 1961, they already had their beliefs which they eventually incorporated into their translation by altering portions of the real Bible that do not support their doctrines.

It is with such a "mis-translated" version of the Bible, they deceive people who give them the room to. My strong appeal here is that, you should not entertain them or listen to them. You cannot argue with them. You cannot convince them no matter what. Their hearts have been seared with a hot iron. So, run from them and do not receive them in your homes. You may need to read this very carefully:

> *Whoever transgresses and does not abide in the doctrine of Christ does not have God. He who abides in the doctrine of Christ has both the Father and the Son (2 John 1:9).*

The doctrine of Christ as used in that passage simply refers to the teachings of Christ which the Jehovah witnesses oppose or condemn today as previously explained. In as much as they do not abide in the doctrine of Christ, we know according to the above scripture that they do not have God. So by welcoming them into your homes you might as well be sharing in their sins.

> *If anyone comes to you and does not bring this doctrine, do not receive him into your house nor greet him; **for he who greets him shares in his evil deeds** (2 John 1:10-11).*

Besides the Jehovah witnesses, there are other religions in the world today that do not believe in the Trinity. For example, Judaism and Islam, as earlier discussed, do not believe that Jesus Christ is God, consequently they condemn, in its entirety, the doctrine of Trinity.

I only wonder why some people cannot use their common sense of reasoning when it comes to religious issues. As human beings, we have been endowed with the ability to reason. One must not believe everything one is told hook, line and sinker. We should be able to analyze issues for ourselves and try to find out if we are on the right path or not.

The Jews, till date, have refused to accept that Jesus was the Messiah, in spite of the fact that Jesus Christ fulfilled the Messianic prophecies as recorded in the books of the prophets. They still therefore endlessly await the birth of the promised Messiah, a prophecy that was fulfilled over two thousand years ago.

In the case of Islam, Muslims do not believe that Jesus Christ is God as a result of what their prophet Muhammad had taught them and as recorded in the Quran. Muhammad may not have written the Quran personally, but all that is recorded in the Quran is credited to him.

Muhammad lived about 600 years after the time of Jesus and yet claimed to have known: how Jesus was born, what He said and did while on earth, whether He died and resurrected or not, whether He ascended into heaven or not, and so on; better than Jesus' disciples who were eye-witnesses to all that actually took place and recorded same. Read Acts 2:32; 5:32; 10:39; 13:31.

This is the disciple who testifies of these things, and wrote these things; and we know that his testimony is true (John 21:24).

And truly Jesus did many other signs in the presence of His disciples, which are not written in this book; but these are written that you may believe that Jesus is the Christ, the Son of God, and that believing you may have life in His name (John 20:30-31).

The point here is that, Jesus did not also personally write the gospels but they were written by His disciples who witnessed everything He said and did while He was with them. My question here is: Why would a logical person prefer to believe an account written after so many years, to the accounts of the eye-witnesses? This I cannot personally understand. If you have ever read parts of the Quran especially where it talks about Jesus Christ, only then you would understand what I am trying to say here.

The Quran gave an account of Jesus Christ that is clearly different from what we read in the Bible as recorded by those who actually witnessed the events; right from His birth till His ascension. For example, the Quran gave an account of Jesus speaking at infancy (few days after His birth) from the cradle (Koran 19:29-33). Muslims also claim that Jesus was never crucified let alone resurrected but that Allah took him to Himself (Koran 3:55).

They however claim that all that is recorded in the Quran was through revelations from Allah (God) via angel Gabriel to Muhammad. If that is true, and Allah is the same as our God, why would such revelations from Allah contradict the previous revelations from God to His prophets of old such as Moses, Isaiah, etc., and the accounts of the eye witnesses in the case of Jesus Christ?

The Quran did not only condemn Christianity, for accepting Jesus as the Son of God, it also condemned the Jews (those who practice Judaism) calling both the "disbelievers." But we know that God is not a man that He should lie or contradict Himself. The words of the Almighty God are yes and Amen and they are forever settled in heaven. Thus God cannot contradict Himself for He is not an author of confusion but of peace.

If all that were actually revealed to him, then I can tell you assuredly that those revelations could not have been from our God (the Christian God). The truth of the matter is that we all have the freedom or free will to believe whatever we want to believe but only the end will tell. However, it might be too late for many to realize the truth by then.

Just as we have read from the gospel above, Jesus is the Messiah, the Son of God. However, the Quran says that Jesus was never the Son of God emphasizing that God can not have a Son or take to Himself a Son. The reason for this is simple. To say that Jesus is the Son of God means that Jesus is God. Since they do not accept that Jesus is

God, they consequently rejected the fact that Jesus is the Son of God emphasizing that there is only one God. But surprisingly, you would find out that the Quran would again make references to Allah as "We." For example:

> "And We have not created the heavens and the earth and that between them except in truth...." (Koran 15:85).

> "And We sent, following in their footstep, Jesus, the son of Mary, confirming that which came before him in the Torah; and We gave him the Gospel......." (Koran 5:46).

From the above verses of the Quran, I guess you would understand my point. The same Quran clearly emphasized that Allah is one and alone, He has no son, no wife, no co-equal, no partner etc., and again used the pronoun "We" for Allah. Just as they have said, if it was Allah (God) that was speaking there, it could therefore mean that Allah also indicated the possibility of the plurality of the Persons in Allah, for Allah being one person, could not have used "We" for himself alone.

Furthermore, a glance at the Quran would reveal to you that the author had access to both the Torah and the Gospel (the complete Bible) as he frequently made references to them, as well as other Biblical events and persons such as Adam, Abraham, Isaac, Jacob, Noah, Moses, John, Mary, Jesus, etc.; and would sometimes debunk biblical facts.

One would have wondered where they got those Biblical knowledge from, but again, it has also been noted that Muhammad's first wife, Khadijah, was a Christian whose Christian cousin, Waraqa, was translating the Gospel to Arabic language at the same time when Muhammad was said to have had the revelations. Thus, one cannot wonder where they would have gotten the knowledge of the Biblical events from, but recorded differently, in the Quran.

A closer look at the Quran attests to the fact that one of the main aims of writing the Quran was to prove that Jesus Christ was neither God nor the Son of God, as it often states "Allah is one and has no son." The Quran even went as far as saying that, Jesus never said He was the Son of God Himself but that it was assumed by the unbelievers. I can only wonder who would have revealed that!

Islam relegates the true position of Christ (calling Him a mere mortal) but exalts Muhammad's position as the last and greatest prophet of God. Thus, one would hear Muslims say: "There is no god but Allah and Muhammad is His prophet." The Quran is primarily against Jesus Christ being God or the Son of God, hence the author negated the Gospel of Christ as we can read today in the Christian Bible, but he again said that the revelations came to confirm the Gospel and the Torah (Koran 2:4; 3:3).

The question however is: Which Gospel did those revelations come to confirm; the Gospel of Christ according to the eye-witnesses (His disciples) or the Gospel of Christ according to Muhammad? This is because I cannot find any confirmation between the two accounts as they are contrasting to each other. For example, we read from the Gospels that Jesus Christ is God and the Son of God but the Quran says otherwise. So, where is the confirmation?

Besides the aforementioned, any other religion that teaches same, as regarding the Divinity of Jesus Christ, claiming that Jesus is not God but a man thereby condemning the doctrine of Trinity, must be treated alike. It is true that other people's religions ought to be respected. However, it is we Christians who respect other religions.

One can hardly attend a church service where the sermon of the day would be based on condemning other religions. But you would find out that, other religions especially Jehovah witnesses, cannot teach their doctrines without first condemning Christianity. They speak evil of what we hold in high esteem, reducing our Lord and Saviour to a mere mortal. Can they do that to other religions?

For example, can the Jehovah witnesses go to the Muslims and speak sacrilege of what the Muslims believe in and hold strongly? Take for instance, that Mohammed is not a prophet? They would not dare that but instead, they look for every opportunity to insult Christianity and everything we believe in, even regarding Christianity (Christendom) as a false religion. It is high time the truth is told!

Having said all that, I am however not surprised because we have been foretold and forewarned by our Lord and Saviour Jesus Christ in the Bible, of the coming of the false Christ or anti-christ and other false prophets and teachers before hand. Let us look at some of the things the Bible says about them:

1   *Then many false prophets will rise up and deceive many (Matt. 24:11).*

2   *Beware of false prophets, who come to you in sheep's clothing, but inwardly they are ravenous wolves (Matt. 7:15).*

3   *False Christ and false prophets will rise and show signs and wonders to deceive, if possible, even the elect. But take heed; see I have told you all things before hands (Mark 13:22 -23).*

4   *False prophets appeared in the past among the people and in the same way, false teacher will appear among you. They will bring in destructive, untrue doctrines and will deny the Master who redeemed them, and so they will bring upon themselves sudden destruction (2 Peter 2:1, GNB).*

5   *Now I urge you, brethren, note those who cause divisions and offences, contrary to the doctrine which you learned,*

and avoid them. For those who are such do not serve our Lord Jesus Christ, but their own belly, and by smooth words and flattering speech deceive the hearts of the simple (Rom. 16:17-18).

6 *Now the spirit expressly says that in latter times some will depart from the faith, giving heed to deceiving spirit and doctrines of demons, speaking lies in hypocrisy, having their own conscience seared with a hot iron (I Tim. 4:1-2).*

7 *Some, having strayed (from true love), have turned aside to idle talk, desiring to be teachers of the law, understanding neither what they say nor the things which they affirm (1 Tim. 1:6-7).*

8 *I marvel that you are turning away so soon from Him who called you in the grace of Christ, to a different Gospel, which is not another; but there are some who trouble you and want to pervert the gospel of Christ (Gal. 1:6-7).*

Note that all these and more were already written in the Bible before their coming. They however still came and are still coming today in order to prove these prophecies right and to fulfill the scriptures. However, the Bible condemns all those who teach or follow false doctrines:

1. *Woe to them! For they have gone in the way of Cain, have run greedily in the error of Balaam for profit, and perished in the rebellion of Korah (Jude 1:11).*

2. *In their greed these false teachers will make a profit out of telling you made-up stories. For a long time now their Judge has been ready and their Destroyer has been wide awake. (2 Peter 2:3 GNB).*

3. *A false witness will not go unpunished, and he who speaks lies shall perish (Prov. 19:9).*

4. *But these, like natural brute beasts made to be caught and destroyed, speak evil of the things they do not understand, and will utterly perish in their own corruption (2 Peter 2:12).*

5. *They shall be punished with everlasting destruction from the presence of the Lord and from the Glory of His power, when He comes, in that Day (2 Thess. 1:9-10).*

6. *For certain men have crept in unnoticed, who long ago were marked out for this condemnation, ungodly men, who turn the grace of our God into lewdness and deny the only Lord God and our Lord Jesus Christ (Jude 1:4).*

7. *The devil, who deceived them, was cast into the lake of fire and brimstone where the beast and the false prophet are. And they will be tormented day and night forever and ever (Rev 20:10).*

No wonder some have already judged themselves that they are not going to heaven but console themselves that there is no hell fire. But from the scriptures, we know that heaven and hell fire are real. Again they regard themselves as the true religion regarding the real Christianity as the false religion as if it was the weed that was sowed first before the wheat.

In the parable of the weed (Matt. 13:24-30), Jesus tells us that a man sowed wheat and only later the enemy came at night and sowed weed among the wheat. Remember, it is the wheat He will gather into His barn; but the chaff or weed He will burn up with unquenchable fire (Matt. 3:12).

However, we have been warned not to follow them and their false teachings:

1. *Therefore let that abide in you which you heard from the beginning. If what you heard from the beginning abides in you, you also will abide in the Son and in the Father. And this is the promise that He has promised – eternal life (1 John 2:24-25).*

2. *But even if we, or an angel from heaven, preach any other gospel to you than what we have preached to you, let him be accursed. As we have said before, so now I say again, if anyone preaches any other gospel to you than what you have received, let him be accursed (Gal. 1:8-9).*

3. *Hold fast the faithful word as you have been taught, that you may be able, by sound doctrine, both to exhort and convict those who contradict (Titus 1:9).*

4. *Watch, stand fast in the faith, be brave, be strong (1 Cor. 16:13).*

5. *Do not be carried about with various and strange doctrines. For it is good that the heart be established by grace, not with foods which have not profited those who have been occupied with them (Heb. 13:9).*

6. *I tell you, then, do not let anyone deceive you with false arguments, no matter how good they seem to be (Col. 2:4 GNB).*

7. *that we should no longer be children, tossed to and fro and carried about with every wind of doctrine, by the trickery of men, in the cunning craftiness of the deceitful plotting, but, speaking the truth in love, may grow up in all things into Him who is the head - Christ (Eph. 4:14).*

He who has ears to hear, Let him hear (Matt.11:15).

CONCLUSION

We have been able to examine the relationship among the Trinitarian God: the Father, the Son and the Holy Spirit. This makes the Christian God different from other religions' gods in that our God is a Trinitarian God or Godhead which consists of the Father, the Son and the Holy Spirit. It is the central doctrine of the Christian faith.

This is why I have earlier noted that our God is different from the Muslim's Allah. You may not have agreed with me on that, as I am aware that a lot of people, virtually all Muslims and some Christians believe that Allah is the same as our Christian God. This is primarily because of the common belief that there is only one God, who created the heaven and the earth.

Therefore, since Allah is called God by Muslims, and believed to have created the universe as well by them, it therefore supposedly means that we are talking about the same Person as God. Just as I had also earlier noted in this book, every religion has its God(s). Thus, Allah is the God of the Islamic religion. That is, Muslims believe in Allah as their God and consequently worship him. That does not necessarily make him our God.

However, I do not know what your personal opinion is concerning this; but again, I would like you to personally examine some facts. From the Gospel, Jesus Christ clearly demonstrated that He was the Son of God. God also confirmed this when He said:

> *"This is My beloved Son, in whom I am well pleased" (Matt. 3:17; 17:5).*

From the above scripture, we as Christians are fully convinced that our God has a Son which is the person of our Lord and Saviour, Jesus Christ. On the other hand, if you read the Quran, then you would find out that Allah also clearly revealed that he does not have a son.

> *Allah is only One God; far be it from His glory that He should have a son (Koran 4:171).*

Therefore, permit me to ask, can our God who has a Son be the same Person as Allah who has no son? Or can our God who revealed and confirmed that He has a Son, be Allah at the same time, who also clearly revealed that he has no son? Does that not clearly substantiate the fact that we are talking about two different "Persons"? How about Jesus Christ being the only way to our God?

Read John 14:6. No one can go to God EXCEPT through Jesus Christ but you would agree with me that, one does not need Jesus Christ to go to Allah just as we do not need Mohammad to go to our God. If Allah is the same as our God, it would mean that one of the two accounts is false (God cannot claim to have a Son and again claim not to have a son!).

The biblical and Koranic accounts about God and Jesus Christ are contrasting (Ironically, the same Quran is said to have been revealed to confirm the pre-existing scriptures). Hence, both cannot be true and correct at the same time. You might be entitled to your own opinion but however let your conclusion be guided by the scripture. Read Galatians 1:8-9.

Having said that, it is important to note that there exists between and among the Trinitarian God a perfect networking relationship: the Father in the Son and the Holy Spirit; the Son in the Father and the Holy Spirit, the Holy Spirit in the Father and the Son. Together they make up one inseparable and indivisible God.

Note that when we say, Jesus Christ is God, we are not only referring to His earthly life but that He was God from the beginning and He is yet God and forever. Again, that Jesus is God does not mean He is God the Father. He is the Son of the Father but both are one God.

It amazes me to hear people say Jesus is not God or cannot be God. If truly you are a Christian who believes in the Bible and the Bible has confirmed that Jesus Christ is God as we have seen, so why is it difficult for you to believe what the Bible says? If it is not written in the Bible, that would have been a different case. So do not even say Jesus is not God or cannot be God but rather that you do not personally believe that He is God. But the good news is that whether you believe or not, that does not change His status as being God because of a truth, He is God.

The divinity of Trinity

The question "Is Jesus Christ God?" I believe, should not be asked by a true Christian (unless asked for specific reasons) but the affirmative statement: Jesus Christ is God! Even when such questions are asked by those who are yet to understand or by non Christians, one must be ready to answer affirmatively: YES, He is God! As well as, educate those who are still ignorant of the fact that Jesus Christ is God.

For me, it is a simple thing to believe in the Divinity of Jesus Christ. He was God, just like the Father, right from the very beginning, lived with God the Father and the Holy Spirit in heaven until He incarnated or came to this earth and lived as a Man, died, resurrected and ascended back to heaven, where He is now seated at the right hand of the Father and lives forever as God.

Even those who limit Him to His earthly life and say He was a mere mortal should also remember that He was conceived and given birth to in a supernatural way of which, has never been heard of anyone before or after Him. The Quran also attests to the fact that Jesus was born of a virgin without the natural process of conception. That alone should have proven to them that Jesus Christ was not just a mere mortal like us. He came down from heaven to earth.

One could also hear some Christians say, besides Jesus there is no other God. Having understood that the three Persons are individually God, do you still believe such statements as: "Besides Jesus there is no other God?"

What about the Father and the Holy Spirit? Do They cease to be God when one says: Besides Jesus there is no other God or that Jesus is the only God? Again I tell you this; Jesus is only one God with the Father and the Holy Spirit. They are one God.

Remember no one can go to God except through Jesus Christ (John 14:6). No one can worship, serve or honour God without worshipping, serving or honouring Jesus Christ (John 5:23). You cannot even claim to believe in God without believing in His Son or claim to have the Father when you do not have the Son (1 John 2:23; 2 John 1:9).

Therefore, we can only glorify God when we glorify His Son. Thus when we say to any of Them: Besides You, there is no other God (whether to the Father, the Son or the Holy Spirit) we are referring to the three Persons at the same time because together They are one God. What it means is that besides Them, there is no other God.

The application of Trinity in our Christian lives implies that the name God encompasses the three divine Persons, the Father, the Son and the Holy Spirit. Therefore when we also pray to God, we should know that we are praying or talking with God the Father, God the Son and God the Holy Spirit at the same time, for They are one.

Whichever of Them you call or pray to, does not matter. What matters is the One in whose Name or through Whom we pray. Jesus said:

The divinity of Trinity

> *Whatever you ask in my Name, I will give it to you (John 14:14).*

And again He said:

> *Whatever you ask the Father in my name, He will give it to you (John 16:23).*

This also shows their oneness.

Whatever we ask in His name, whether from the Father or the Son in faith and according to God's will, we would be given. The most important thing is the name JESUS, a name which is above every other name. At the mention of the name of Jesus, every knee must bow and every tongue must confess that Jesus is Lord. Whoever shall call upon the name of the Lord shall be saved, for there is no other name known among men through whom we are saved.

Having said all of these, I believe we can now convincingly say that the Father is God, the Son is God and the Holy Spirit is God and that the Three make up our God. Thus, **THE HOLY TRINITY**.

May the Grace of our Lord Jesus Christ, the Love of God and the Fellowship of the Holy Spirit be with us all forever and ever, Amen.

REFERENCES

Note that this book is a Biblical perspective of the subject matter. As such, its main reference is the Holy Bible hence various Translations or Versions of the Bible were used as can be seen from the Abbreviation list.

However other sources include:

Michael E. Bassey, The Bible Says (Volume 1), 1997.

Smith Wigglesworth, Smith Wigglesworth on the Holy Spirit, 1999

A Catechism of the Christian Doctrine, 1971.

Bible Dictionary (New Century Version), 2003.

The Oxford Advanced Learner's Dictionary, 2010.

The Catechism of the Catholic Church, 1992.

The Quran.

The Jehovah Witness New World Translation.

Wikipedia (The free encyclopedia, online).

The Catholic Encyclopedia (online).

And other internet sources.